COUNT MICHAEL MAIER

ÆTATIS
SVÆ 49.
A 1617.

TRES SCHOLA, TRES COESAR TITVLOS DE=
DIT; HÆC MIHI RESTANT,
POSSE BENE IN CHRISTO VIVERE, POSSE MORI.
MICHAEL MAIERVS COMES IMPERIALIS CON=
SISTORII etc. PHILOSOPH· ET MEDICINARVM
DOCTOR. P. C. C. NOBIL. EXEMPTVS FOR·OLIM
MEDICVS CÆS. etc.

COUNT MICHAEL MAIER

Doctor of Philosophy and of Medicine
Alchemist, Rosicrucian, Mystic

1568–1622

Life and Writings

*"Adamum hunc Lapidem secum portasse e Paradyso, et quemlibet eum
secum habere, in me, in te, et in quolibet alio"*—ut Morienus ait.

—"Verum Inventum," *p. 87.*

Rev. J. B. Craven, D. D.

Foreword by R. A. Gilbert

Ibis Press
An Imprint of Nicolas-Hays, Inc.
Berwick, Maine

First published in 2003 by
Ibis Press
An Imprint of Nicolas-Hays, Inc.
P. O. Box 1126
Berwick, ME 03901-1126
www.nicolashays.com

Distributed by Red Wheel/Weiser LLC
Box 612
York Beach, ME 03901-0612
www.redwheelweiser.com

Cataloging-in-Publication Data available by request at the
Library of Congress

Cover design by Phillip Augusta
Typeset in Century Expanded 10/14; display type:
Charlemagne

Printed in the United States of America
VG

CONTENTS.

ERRATA.

Pages 7 and 114—For " Silentio " read " Silentium.
Page 96—For " Symbolum " read " Symbola."

"ALL THINGS ARE DOUBLE, ONE AGAINST ANOTHER: AND HE HATH MADE NOTHING IMPERFECT."

—*Ecclus., xlii. 24.*

FOREWORD

HEN the Reverend Dr. J. B. Craven published his book *Doctor Robert Fludd* one hundred years ago, he intended it to be the first in a trilogy of studies on the spiritual alchemists. The third study, of Heinrich Khunrath, did not appear until long after Craven's death,[1] but it was his second book on these enigmatic men that was the most important. *Count Michael Maier* was published in 1914, but it is still "The only comprehensive monograph on Fludd's associate"[2] in English. It would be foolish to set any one of Craven's three subjects above the others in terms of their significance in the field of alchemical art, but Maier was the most prolific author, and Craven's is the only study to analyze all of his works in depth.

Craven was a deep student of alchemical texts and was well aware that alchemy operates on two levels. Material alchemy is concerned with the pursuit of a tincture that will transmute base metals into gold, the most precious metal of all, and with the parallel quest of an elixir that will grant

---

[1] *Doctor Heinrich Khunrath. A Study in Mystical Alchemy.* Hermetic Studies Series. No. 1. 141 pp., with fourteen illustrations (Glasgow, 1997).

[2] Joscelyn Godwin, *Robert Fludd: Hermetic Philosopher and Surveyor of Two Worlds* (Boulder, 1979), p. 94

health and immortality, or at least extreme longevity, to
the alchemist. But even if the possibility is admitted that
the goals of physical alchemy may not be chimerical, their
pursuit is, ultimately, futile. The most casual reflection will
bring the realization that physical immortality, however
wealthy one may be, is not a blessing but a curse. Spiritual
alchemy, however, is another matter.

Fludd, Maier, and Khunrath were all physicians, alive
to the frailty of the human body, and without any illusions
as to the uncomfortable closeness of death. They did not
reject the potential merits of the laboratory, but their
prime concern was with spiritual alchemy: a symbolic
expression of the quest for the regeneration of the human
spirit and its ultimate reintegration with God. The symbols
used to illustrate this quest may be verbal or pictorial,
but as the language of alchemy is obscure and frequently
paradoxical, most of the spiritual alchemists, including the
three studied by Craven, made extensive use of pictorial
imagery. Their most important works are built around
exquisite drawings of great complexity, finely engraved
with a technical skill that brings out the minutest detail.

These alchemists were well served by the engravers
who worked for them, but their own skill lies not only in
this wealth of imagery, but in the painstaking descriptions
and interpretations of the images that are set down in the
written texts. To a certain degree, alchemical engravings
are modeled on the engraved emblem books that were
highly popular in the 16th and 17th centuries. But the
emblem books serve an essentially moral purpose. They
guide the reader, with the aid of engraved pictures, through
the moral maze of this world, and provide a reminder that
it is by faith and adherence to the moral law that the reader
will attain to heaven in the next life.

The approach of the spiritual alchemist is different: the spiritual alchemist seeks to convey to the student of his or her texts and images the nature and practical application of a process that can, and may, lead the student to the direct experience of God in this life. But while the spiritual alchemist may seek, he or she does not always succeed in conveying the intended message. Much depends on the understanding and dedication of the student, who is expected to be of high moral character, well-instructed in biblical, classical, and contemporary literature, so that he or she can understand the many allusions made, in both words and pictures, in alchemical texts and dedicated to the spiritual life.

Canon Craven did fulfill these requirements, but most of us will fall short of that ideal. We need a guide to explain the explanations of the alchemists, so that we also may be able to pierce the veil of the pictorial symbolism and paradoxical language of their texts. This is what Craven attempts to provide for the work of Fludd, Maier, and Khunrath. Whether or not he succeeds is a matter for the individual reader to determine, but it is undeniable that he skillfully avoids the danger of burying the words and images of the alchemists under another layer of text. In his book on Fludd, and even more so in his study of Maier, Canon Craven accurately describes and meticulously analyzes their works without recourse to reproductions of the engravings, the inclusion of which would have made his books prohibitively expensive.

Today we are fortunate in having easy access to a vast range of alchemical engravings through such books as Johannes Fabricius' *Alchemy: The Medieval Alchemists and their Royal Art* (Copenhagen, 1976) and Stanislaus Klossowski de Rola's *The Golden Game: Alchemical*

Engravings of the Seventeenth Century (London, 1988).
De Rola includes illustrations from nine of Maier's works,
while the entire series of engravings from *Atalanta
Fugiens* is reproduced in H.M.E. de Jong, *Michael Maier's
Atalanta Fugiens: Sources of an Alchemical Book of
Emblems* (York Beach, 2002)

Craven was more fortunate in that he examined copies
of seventeen of Maier's works in their original editions;
some in institutional or private libraries in England and
Scotland, and eight in his own remarkable collection.
That his own library also included more recent works on
alchemy is clear from Craven's introduction. He evidently
possessed copies of both *A Suggestive Inquiry into the
Hermetic Mystery* (1850) and E. A. Hitchcock's *Remarks
upon Alchemy and the Alchemists* (1857). These were
seminal texts for the perception of alchemy as a spiritual
pursuit, and they may have been the source of Craven's
lifelong enthusiasm for the subject.

His comments on the *Suggestive Inquiry* also suggest
that while he was thoroughly versed in the text, he
was ill-informed about the author, for he turns Thomas
South into a clergyman and converts his daughter—Mrs.
Atwood—into his sister! But such minor faults in his work[3]
did not prevent him from gaining public recognition—
eventually. *Count Michael Maier* received little critical
notice on publication. No reviews appeared *The Occult*

---

[3] One "error," rather a reflection of mistaken opinion by
Craven, is interesting, He disputes A. E. Waite's contention
that *Arcana Arcanissima* was printed at London, and goes
with the "best authorities" in believing it to have been
issued at Oppenheim. Recent research has vindicated Waite
(see de Rola, *The Golden Game*, p. 60).

Review, *The Quest*, or *Light*, but the book was certainly known to A. E. Waite, Dr. Westcott, Isabelle de Steiger, Professor Ferguson and H. S. Redgrove, who were the leading English writers on alchemy at the time. When the Alchemical Society was founded, in 1913, Canon Craven was soon elected an Honorary Vice-President "in recognition of his services to the study of alchemical literature by the publication of digests of the writings of Robert Fludd and Michael Maier."[4]

Presumably delighted with the honor bestowed, and undeterred by the seeming faint praise—both books are far more than more "digests"—Craven took his membership seriously and produced two papers for the society, although difficulties of travel from the Orkney Islands prevented his attendance at any of the meetings in London. The first paper, "A Scottish Alchemist of the Seventeenth Century: David, Lord Balcarres," was read by the secretary, W. Gorn Old ("Sepharial"), at the May meeting in 1913. It reflects Craven s continuing interest in those alchemists who were also concerned with Rosicrucianism. The second paper, "Alchemy and the Devil," delivered in February 1915 at one of the society's last meetings before it succumbed to the turmoil of WWI, was more unusual and provoked considerable comment, especially from the lady members of the society.

It also seems probable that membership in the Alchemical Society led Canon Craven to the truth about the authorship of *A Suggestive Inquiry*. He would have come to know, if he did not already know, Isabelle de Steiger and her books, and would also have received the premature

---

4   *Journal of the Alchemical Society* 1, part 3 (March 1913): 33.

publicity brochure[5] about the reprint of Mrs. Atwood's book. This quotes both his own comments on Dr. South and Mme. de Steiger's more accurate account of the book's history. However, by the time that the reprint finally appeared, in 1918, the publisher had parted company with Isabelle de Steiger and replaced her "Biographical Memoir" with an introduction by W. L. Wilmshurst. This contains a sneering reference to the Alchemical Society, dismissing its efforts toward establishing a canon of criticism for alchemical texts as futile, and condemning the membership for showing "no comprehension of [alchemy's] vital intention or its practical methods" (p. 62). For Craven's work, this was an especially unjust remark.

His paper on "Alchemy and the Devil" shows the breadth of his reading and learning and indicates that he kept fully up to date with the literature of all branches of esoteric study, not only with alchemy. What led him to this branch of the Western Hermetic Tradition, and when, is unknown. If it was *A Suggestive Inquiry*, then the question remains: Why did he fix upon so rare and obscure a book?

Too little is recorded of Craven's life to provide a certain answer, but a pattern of interests does emerge. James Brown Craven was born in 1850 into a clerical family. He was ordained in the Scottish Episcopal Church in 1875, although he was not a Scot, and served as a curate in Aberdeen for one year until he was instituted as Rector of St. Olaf's Church at Kirkwall on the Orkney Islands. He held this post until 1913 when he was appointed to the post of Archdeacon of Orkney. His studies of Scottish

---

[5]   This is of 8 pp., issued by the publisher, William Tait of Belfast, but undated. It was probably printed in 1912 and sent out for some time afterward.

church history were held in high regard and gained him an honorary Doctorate in Divinity from the University of Aberdeen. None of this was a necessary preparation for esoteric pursuits, but it should be noted that the Scottish Episcopal Church leans toward advanced ritual and a "high" liturgy.

Given his enthusiasm for elaborate ceremonial, it is not surprising that Canon Craven should have been initiated into Freemasonry. Soon after arriving in Kirkwall, he became a member of Lodge Kirkwall Kilwinning No. 38² and wrote the first account of the famous Kirkwall Scroll: a linen scroll some eighteen feet in length, painted with biblical scenes and much Masonic imagery. In his description, Craven does not attempt to date the scroll, although his references to specific Masonic degrees necessitate a mid- to late 18th-century origin, which is now accepted as correct.[6] He was an active mason, attaining high office in Craft Masonry,[7] and in February 1887 he became one of the earliest members of the Correspondence Circle of Quatuor Coronati Lodge of Research. This would have brought him within the orbit of W. J. Hughan, Wynn Westcott, F. G. Irwin and other enthusiasts for esoteric Freemasonry, although there is no evidence that Craven joined any of the fringe Masonic bodies; nor does he seem to have become a member of either

---

[6] The article, "Kirkwall Kilwinning Lodge No. 38² and its remarkable Scroll," was published in *Ars Quatuor Coronatorum* 10 (1897): 79–81.

[7] He was appointed as Deputy Provincial Grand Master for the Province of Caithness, Orkney, and Zetland. This is the approximate equivalent to a Deputy Insider Grand Master in American Masonry but the office is usually held for a much longer period of time in Britain.

the English or Scottish Masonic Rosicrucian Societies.

But lack of membership did not mean lack of interest. Craven was well aware of the significance of Michael Maier in the birth and growth of the Rosicrucian movement. Of the three works by Maier relevant to Rosicrucianism, he discusses *Themis Aurea*, the most important of them, in depth and provides brief overviews of the others: *Silentium Post Clamores* and *Symbola Aurea*. Craven accepts that Maier was a Rosicrucian and that he introduced Robert Fludd to the fraternity, thus going against the prevailing skeptical view as to the reality of any Rosicrucian fraternity in the material world. Long after Craven's death, his faith in Maier has been vindicated.

In 1979 Adam McLean published an account of "A Rosicrucian Manuscript of Michael Maier,"[8] in which he described a document on parchment that is an elaborate greetings card addressed to King James VI and I. It was presented by Maier to King James, at Christmas 1611, on behalf of Frederick, the Elector Palatine who was then a suitor for the Princess Elizabeth. Their subsequent marriage, in February 1613, created a political alliance between two important Protestant nations, with the possibility of wresting Bohemia from the strongly Catholic successor to the benign and esoterically inclined Emperor Rudolf. It also seems probable, from the tone of their manifestos of 1614 and 1613, that the Rosicrucians— whoever they may have been—actively sought to promote this scenario.

---

[8] In *The Hermetic Journal*, No. 5, (Autumn, 1979): 4–7. The article includes an illustration of the rose and cross, redrawn from the original manuscript.

From 1617 onwards Maier had actively promoted the Rosicrucians in print. He had also been physician to the Emperor Rudolf until his death in 1612, in which year he visited Britain, where he met fellow physicians, including Robert Fludd and Sir William Paddy who was physician to King James. Now it is clear that he had been supporting Frederick's, and thus the Rosicrucians' cause even earlier. But can we legitimately describe the "Christmas greetings" manuscript as Rosicrucian? We can, for it contains a cross of gold letters superimposed on a red rose of eight petals, and there are allusions to the Rose and Cross in the words around the petals. In addition, four poems flank the rose, one of which is titled "The Chorus of the Angels Gabriel, Raphael, Uriel, Michael." The association with esoteric Christianity—more precisely, with *Reformed esoteric* Christianity—is abundantly clear. And there is more: The poems are accompanied by music.

The use of music was crucial for Maier. In *Atalanta Fugiens*, the emblematic engravings are related to the epigrams, which are designed to be sung as three-part fugues. In his edition of the book (Magnum Opus Hermetic Sourceworks No. 22, 1987) Joscelyn Godwin makes the case for Maier having intended his work to be treated as an integral whole. This is alchemy as spiritual practice: singing the epigrams while reflecting on the pictorial content of the relevant emblem employs both voice and vision to create a mood conducive to working toward exalted spiritual experience.

It is not, nor is it intended to be, an easy practice. Unlike simple contemplation of the pictorial emblems—which can lead us astray into sentimental reverie—this process of absorption into the whole setting requires discipline, concentration, and dedication. The end result is eminently worthwhile. Canon Craven did not emphasize Maier's music, but he noted that "all the alchemical processes signified stages on the road to this perfection," which is "arrival at the 'perfect work'"—the reintegration of Human in God. This is the true gold and goal of the spiritual alchemists, of whom Michael Maier is perhaps the perfect exemplar. If we seek to follow the path that he points out for us, then we can ask for no better text than J. B. Craven's book to guide us through the complexities of Maier's works and bring us to a proper understanding of them. And then our real work will begin.

R. A. GILBERT
Bristol, October 2003

LIFE OF MICHAEL MAIER.

ALL authorities agree that Michael Maier was born at Rendsburg, in Holstein, about the year 1568. The date is taken from the inscription on his portrait as prefixed to his "Symbola," "Atalanta fugiens," and "Septimana Philosophica." The picture was painted in 1617, when he was forty-nine years of age. In one of his dedications to Frederick, Count of Holstein, he refers to the fact that "my family is well known, not only by all the nobility of Holstein, but also to your highness' father and grandfather, to whose service mine have always been faithfully attached." Rendsburg is a town on the north side of the now famous Baltic Canal, nineteen miles west of Kiel, with a population of some 15,000. Unfortunately, the Church records extend only to the seventeenth century, and therefore can yield us no information as to the birth of Maier.

On the other hand, a John Meyer or Meyger was a church official in Rendsburg in 1541—an old Lutheran clergyman in 1577. Others are found bearing the same name. There was a Grithoffe Meyer or Meyger, a revenue officer in Rendsburg—that is a tax-collector for the landed proprietors; also a John Meyer, who was a district official on the west coast—a dyke inspector.[1]

Michael Maier himself tells us that he left Holstein in 1608. It was his desire to return to end his days in his native province, but his almost premature death prevented

[1] Information from Herr R. R. von Lilienstern, first Burgomaster of Rendsburg.

B

this being accomplished. After graduating in medicine, we find him at Rostock. Beyond the fact that he appears to have graduated at that university, the archives of Rostock throw no light upon his history.[1]

At anyrate, he soon proved himself to be a man of distinction, and came under the notice of the Emperor Rudolph II. He was appointed a body physician to the Emperor. Rudolph, the son of Maximilian II. and of Maria of Austria, daughter of Charles V., was born in Vienna in 1552. His mother gave him an ardent zeal for the Roman Church, which feeling was strengthened by his early residence in Spain. Rudolph was crowned Emperor and King of Hungary in 1572, and King of Bohemia in 1575. Lutheranism had considerably increased through the allowance of Maximilian, and although Rudolph confirmed his father's privileges granted to noble Protestants, yet he banished some of their preachers and restricted their meetings. Rudolph resided at Prague, to which he summoned Maier, enobled him, making him Pfalzgraf—Count Palatine—and his private secretary. The Emperor, who was devoted to science, invited to his court the celebrated Tycho Brahe, who was greatly attached to the practices of judicial astrology and alchemy. His prognostics warned Rudolph that he would suffer great danger through a prince of his own blood. He began to lose affection for his own family, and to elude all propositions for marriage. Ceasing to show himself in public, he had covered galleries constructed in order to pass into his gardens, from a fear of assassination. He surrounded himself with "astrologers, chemists, painters, turners, engravers, mechanicians, and amused himself with his botanic gardens, his cabinets of natural history and galleries of antiquities." In 1611, Matthias, his brother, arrived at Prague, when Rudolph, having called a diet, offered to resign the crown to his brother on account of his advanced age, and then dispensed his subjects from their oaths of fidelity. Matthias being

[1] Information from Dr Kohfeldt, Librarian of Rostock University.

crowned with great magnificence, Rudolph then retired to one of his pleasure houses. He was eventually allowed to inhabit the palace at Prague, and had a pension of 400,000 florins. Vexed and humiliated by what he had undergone, his sedentary life brought him to the tomb in the 60th year of his age and in the 37th year of his reign—20th January 1612. Rudolph was a man of elegant manners, affability, and easy conversation. He possessed a great knowledge of languages, both ancient and modern, and was skilled in painting and mechanical arts, in botany, zoology, and chemistry. " His century and his country owed much to this love of science and art, which caused his misfortune. His court was filled with artists and men of eminent merit. Kepler was employed conjointly with Tycho Brahe to arrange the calendars, which have thence received the name of Rudolphine. He also formed superb collections, and many of his precious stones, antiques, and pictures are now among the finest ornaments of the cabinets of Vienna." [1]

Maier does not appear, however, to have been in constant attendance on the Emperor. In 1611, he tells us he was at Amsterdam, where he saw a superb collection of shells in the cabinet of a Dutch antiquary. After the death of Rudolph, Maier visited England, where he made the acquaintance of Doctor Robert Fludd, Sir William Paddy, Sir Thomas Smith, and Francis Anthony.

Maier's first publication was his "Arcana Arcanissima," which he dedicated to Sir William Paddy, physicion to King James I. of England, a fellow of St John's College, Oxford, a graduate in medicine of Leyden, afterwards President of the College of Physicians of London, the friend of Laud, and a benefactor to St John's." [2] The "Arcana" bears no date, but is generally believed to have been printed about the year 1614.

Morhof, in his Polyhistor, referring to the opinions held by Faber and Vignerius, that the chymic doctrine was

[1] Dic. Univ. Biog., *in voce*.   [2] Dic. Nat. Biog., xliii. 35.

hidden or embodied in many ancient inscriptions, adds that
Maier advances this doctrine in his "Arcana," although he
thinks (rightly) that in some respects he seems to read
more into the inscriptions and hieroglyphics than can be
actually found in them. As illustrating the views put
forward by Maier in the "Arcana," a MS. written by him
may be mentioned. It is still preserved in the library of
the University of Leipzig, and bears the title, " Tractatus
de Theosophia Ægyptiorum ab antiquissima sic abdita
sacra." It is believed that this is the only MS. in Maier's
writing which has survived the destruction of Magdeburg.[1]

The writer has to thank the Rev. E. F. Scofield, B.D.,
lately British chaplain at Leipzig, for the following interesting description of this MS. He writes :—" It consists of
130 sheet = 260 pages, including title page and blank
back of ditto ; size of paper = $6\frac{1}{2}$ × $8\frac{3}{8}$ in. Sheets are
written in small, neat hand on both sides—doubtless easily
legible to experienced eye, but to me somewhat difficult to
decipher. The ink is for the most part well preserved ;
paper strongly yellow. The binding is merely paper of the
same nature apparently as paper of body of book, with an
extra large sheet of a sort of pergament paper folded over
same, much as one covers a book in reading to protect
cover. This outer wrapper bears the title which you have
given me, fairly distinct, i.e., 'Tractatus de Theosophia
Ægyptiorum ab antiquissima sic abdita sacra.' There
follows a good deal of writing, but in consequence of water
or some stain, this is quite illegible. The title page outside
cover reads thus :—' De circulo artium Coelidonia Medicina
Mystica, &c. Hæc de Lapide sanitatis, philosophia, &c.
Tractatus Hermeticus quo Diversas artes et Disciplinas ex
una Ægytiorum antiquissimorum chemia, tanquam fonte,
pro fluxine demonstratus, et antiquitas ejus ad laudem Dei

---

[1] The mention of a MS. by Maier in the University of Leyden by Mr
Yarker, in his "Arcane Schools" (p. 212), is a mistake. The Librarian of
Leyden University assures the writer that " Leyden " was mistaken for
" Leipzig."

Opt. Max. nee non utilitatem hominis clarissima afferitur, authore, Michaele Mayero Phil. et Med. D., &c.' [sic.]

" Inside first page of cover is a short note, apparently in a somewhat later but *not* recent hand, which, so far as I could decipher, reads thus :—' Eadem . . . Mich. Meiero in Arcana Arcanissima sive Hieroglyph. Ægypto-Græc. Vulgo nondum cognitur. Eum sequntur in hoc instituto vize . . . Commentario in Philosoph. Tabulas et Peter (?) Joh. Faber in Paro (? Pavo) chymico suo V. Norhof . . . cept de Transmut. metall. p. 103, 104, 105.'

" The title page is followed by preface, but so far as I can make it out, there are no details of any sort *re* Maier's own personality, nor is any such appended at end. It concludes with a loose leaf, which appears to be brief annotations or supplementary remarks relating to statements in the body of the MS."

The dedication to Sir William Paddy of the "Arcana" is printed on an engraved page, but Maier seems to have had some copies thrown off with the dedication omitted, in place of which he inserted in manuscript inscriptions to various friends. One of these has been preserved, and as it is believed that the writing is in Maier's own hand, a facsimile is given of the page. It bears the inscription :—
" To the Right Worshipful and most Worthy favourer of all vertues, Sir Thomas Smith, Knight, &c., Michael Maierus, Med. D., &c., author, wisheth much health and prosperous felicitie, and al increase of worship in this life, &c." [1] This Sir Thomas Smith was " so much in favour with K. James that he sent him ambassador to the Emperor of Russia, 19 March 1604." He was first governor of the East India Company, and treasurer of the Virginia Company. " He built a fair, magnificent house at Deptford, near London." In the year 1612, he was " prime undertaker for that noble design, the discoverie of the North-West passage." In his later age he retired from public life, and lies buried in the church of Sutton-at-Hone,

---

[1] Through the kindness of J. Rosenthal, of Munich.

Kent, where his stately monument, inclosed with iron
rails, may still be seen—

> " To this obscured village he with drewe ;
> From thence his heavenlie voiage did persue ;
> Here summ'd up all."

Sir Thomas Smith died 4th April 1625.[1]

Another English friend was Francis Anthony. To him
(along with two other friends) is inscribed Maier's " Lusus
Serius." The dedication is dated at Frankfort, " ex Anglia
reditu, Pragam abituriens anno 1616, Mense Septembri."
These three friends are described as most wise doctors of
medicine, expert chemists, and his most jocund friends.
Francis Anthony was a graduate of Cambridge, and son
of a goldsmith in London. He " pretended to be the first
discoverer and to make known to the world a ' medicine
called Aurum Potabile.' " This discovery caused considerable stir, and a number of pamphlets appeared for and
against. This Dr Anthony died " in St Bartholomew's
Close (where he had lived many years) on 26th May 1623,
and was buried in the isle joining to the north side of the
chancel of St Bartholomew the Great in London." He
appears to have been a student and rather a recluse, but
" a great Paracelsian." [2]

But the most distinguished friend in England whom
Maier had was the famous Doctor Robert Fludd. How
they became acquainted we do not know, but it appears
that when in England Maier " lived on friendly terms "
with Fludd. It is said that it was at Maier's instigation
Fludd wrote, or at least published, in 1617 his most
excellent " Tractatus Theologo-Philosophicus," dedicated to
the brethren of the Rosy Cross.

We are told that Maier, having become a member of
this mysterious order, admitted Fludd to its privileges
when in England. The whole matter is, however, buried

---

[1] Wood's "Athenæ," ii. 54, 55.

[2] Wood's "Athenæ," ii. 416 ; Aubrey's "Lives," i. 32. For Dr
Anthony's recipe for the "Aurum Potabile," see " Collectanea Chemica,"
1893. It is entirely chemical.

TO THE
RIGHT WORSHIPFVL AND
most Worshipfull favourer of
all worthie SIR THO-
MAS SMITH, Knight

in obscurity, if not in contradiction. In addition to the publication of the " Themis Aurea," a number of references to the Rosicrucian mystery will be found in Maier's works. There is, of course, the " Silentio," and in the " Symbola " he gives an account and defence of the society. A number of offered doubts are there proposed and answered. He defends the genuineness of the " Confessio," innumerable editions of which, and of the " Fama," have appeared. The " Fama " was issued in English by Thomas Vaughan in 1663, but as early as 1633, it had been translated into " braid Scots," an edition still in MS., but which I should like greatly to have printed, with some notes on earlier esoteric studies in Scotland. The idea of the society took hold on many minds, and its occult and mysterious nature (yet abiding) seemed to appeal to members who were both learned and devout. Fludd's " Apologia " is said to have been written at the instigation or request of Maier. It was published at Leyden in 1616, and again in 1617.[1]

With the exception of the " Lusus Serius " and the " Themis Aurea," none of Maier's works have been translated into English. The " Lusus," of which the English edition is extremely rare, was issued in our language in 1654, translated by Robert Hegge—" a prodigy of his time for forward and good natural parts "—a native of Durham. " Half of which almost was done in one afternoon over a glass of wine in a tavern." [2]

Maier is said to have been wiled away from the practical path he had long followed by " some adepts," and become greatly enamoured of the discovery of the alchemic secret in its lower forms. It is said that " he scoured all Germany to hold conferences with those whom he thought to be in possession of transcendent secrets."

---

[1] Those who wish to pursue this subject further may consult the able paper (and authorities) by Dr Wynn Westcott in the "Ars Quat. Coron.," vii. 36., et seq. ; and my " Life and Writings of Dr Robert Fludd."
[2] Wood's "Athenæ," ii. 460.

Another account declares that he sacrificed his health, his fortune, and his time in these " ruinous absurdities." [1]

In 1619 he became physician to the Landgrave Moritz of Hesse, to whom he had, in 1616, from Frankfort, dedicated his little treatise, " De Circulo." But eventually he settled and practised medicine at Magdeburg, whence, in 1620, he issued his " Septimana Philosophica. It is dedicated to Christian Wilhelm, postulated Archbishop of Magdeburg and Primate of Germany, to whose celsitude he pays the deepest reverence, and subscribes himself his most obedient subject and servant. The date of this dedication is Magdeburg, 11th Jan. (old style) 1620. In August 1620, he dates the dedication of his " Civitas Corporis humani " from the same city. The volume was issued at Frankfort in 1621.

Maier was not destined to return and end his days in Holstein. He died at Magdeburg in 1622, " tempore Æstivo." We are told by his friend who published his " Ulysses " in 1624, that he passed away " piously," and before his death gave into the hands of his friend that little treatise. It is added that he was a regular attendant at the house of God, a Christian in life and conversation, and that he practised that charity exhibited in the person of Christ as shown in the parable of the good Samaritan.

The writer has taken every measure to ascertain if any monument to Maier exists at Magdeburg. Unfortunately, all the official records of that city were destroyed in the great fire of 1631. The present authorities of the cathedral state " that so far as they know, Michael Maier was not buried in the cathedral," at anyrate, " they have no trace of his tomb." [2] The history of the destruction of the city of Magdeburg is well known. In 1629 it was vainly beseiged for six months by Wallenstein, but in May 1631, after a heroic defence (2000 against 25,000), it was taken

---

[1] Waite, " Real History of the Rosicrucians," 268.
[2] Information kindly communicated by Mr Edgar Drake, British Vice-Consul at Magdeburg.

by Tilly and burned to the ground, the cathedral (re-
consecrated to Roman Catholic worship) being almost all
that remained after the three days' sack in which nearly
the whole population of 36,000 perished by fire, sword, or
drowning in the river Elbe. In 1646, the archbishopric
was converted into a secular duchy.

In religion, Maier appears to have been a devout
Lutheran. In his " Munera" there are several severe
attacks upon the Roman Church and Court. In the
" Symbola" he gives some account of what were apparently his impressions of the Church of England. He
refers to the disuse of images and other ancient symbols
of religion. These were in a great measure retained by
the Lutherans. He asks on what grounds the Church of
England has cast down and rejected the statues of the
saints, while preserving the figures of the Lion and
Unicorn in her places of Divine worship.

It is to be regretted that the materials for a life of
Maier are so scanty and elusive. Much must have perished in the sack of Magdeburg. Yet the best memorials
are those in his writings, the " Symbola" and " Atalanta
fugiens" particularly.

His works contain, says Langlet de Fresnoy, " much
curious material, and I am astonished that the German
booksellers, who publish innumerable worthless works,
have not condescended to perceive that a complete collection of the writings of Michael Maier would be more
useful, and command a larger sale, than the trash with
which they overwhelm scholars and the public generally." [1]
It is much to be wished that the two works mentioned
above, supplemented by the " Ulysses," were translated
into English and published for the use of students. An
explanatory key to some portions of the " Atalanta" would
show readers how deep, how wonderful, and how learned
were Maier's researches.

[1] Quoted by Waite, " Real Histy.," 249.

Some references to the opinions and criticisms of others may not be unsuitable.

Fludd, no doubt, was as deeply learned as Maier—more extensively so, perhaps. But his studies were different. They were anatomical, cabalistic, in Jewish and Christian theology. Maier, again, excelled in classical and profane learning. He had a thorough knowledge of all ancient mythology, particularly of Egypt as then known, and of Greece. The lives in the " Symbola " are really the mines from which subsequent writers have imperfectly equipped themselves. These lives are the sources from which many later authors have drawn many curious stories and quaint anecdotes of the times and doings of the ancient alchemists and nature students. Maier did not profess to be a theologian. Fludd was one. Both types were united in a third, Henry Khunrath, whose " Amphitheatrum," and " Chaos " deserve more study than they have received.

Putting aside for the time Rosicrucian stories and disputes, let us try to gather some moral and religious lessons from these three great students.

There is no treatise which breathes more love, warm and devout, to Jehovah, Greatest and Best, than the " Tractatus Theologo-Philosophicus" of Robert Fludd. The same devout spirit may be seen, though perhaps in a stiffer form, in Maier's " Ulysses."

There appears to have been little learning then known which was not studied and assimilated by Maier. He had, no doubt, great opportunities at Prague. The library of Rudolph was immense, choice, complete. Fludd's reading is, perhaps, more restricted, and Khunrath's mostly Scriptural. Yet these three complete the circle, and reveal to us eager souls, determined to master antiquity—Classic, Jewish, and Christian. Perhaps the " Ulysses," the last note struck by Maier, is the apex. After all his adventures, the great hero of antiquity returns home, there finding love and rest. Astute, eloquent, prudent, ingenious in labour, in war, in danger, ever constant and true,

Ulysses is to Maier the symbol of perfect human manhood and wisdom, that wisdom which adorns manners, gains riches, and tempers virtues.

That Maier was a searcher after the actual stone and tincture, there can be little doubt. In parts of his writings this seems clear enough. He believed (as many did) in the transmutation of metals, in the art of multiplying gold. These old naturalists believed that metals grew like plants, and therefore could be cultivated from seed. They sought to find this seed. Some believed that they did find it. Maier was not free from this gold fever, nor was Khunrath. They desired riches, and that desire at times may have drawn Maier away from higher studies. Yet the most precious gold which they all sought, the wine of the wise— these were not merely material. They really are seeking, sometimes groping after, the real experiment of Nature. In a measure they succeeded. Perhaps in this Maier stands on the lower level. His conception of the Rosicrucian Society, with all its secrets, is not a high one, nor a mysterious one. In his "Themis Aurea," the brethren appear merely as hard-working students of Nature, physicians and chemists. They "have alwaies had one among them as cheefe and governor, to whom they are obedient. They have the true astronomy, the true physicke, mathematicks, medicine, and chymistry by which they are able to produce rare and wonderful effects. They are very laborious, frugall, temperate, secret, and true."

References to Maier will be found in the following works :—

Van der Linden, " De Scriptis Libri Duo," 1637, p. 362.
Borel, " Bibliotheca Chimica," 1654, pp. 149-153, 267.
Morhof, " De Metallorum Transmutatione Epistola," 1673, pp. 84, 104, 146.
König, " Bibliotheca Vetus et Nova," 1678, p. 496.
Mercklin, " Lindenius Renovatus," 1686, p. 817.
Manget, " Bibliotheca Scriptorum Medicorum," 1731, ii., i., p. 128.
" Jacob Leupolds Prodromus," 1732, p. 96.
Morhof, " Polyhistor," 1732, i., p. 106, 123 ; ii., pp. 169, 422, 434, 444 ; iii., p. 554.

12   COUNT MICHAEL MAIER.

Kestner, " Med. Gelehrten-Lexicon," 1740, p. 503.
Arnold, Kirchen und Ketzer-Historien, 1741, Bd. ii., p. 253 (Th.
    ii., B. xvii., c., xviii., sec. 24), Bd. iii., A. p. 116, sec. 3.
Lenglet Dufresnoy, " Hist. de la Phil. Hermetique," 1742, i., pp.
    384, 477 ; iii., pp., 47, 48, 225-230, 284.
Moller, " Cimbria Literata," Havniæ, 1744, i., pp. 376-380.
Vogt, " Catalogus Historico-Criticus Librorum Rariorum," Ed.
    3rd, 1747, p. 430.
Jöcher, "Allgemeines Gelehrten-Lexicon," 1751, iii., col. 329 ;
    Rotermund's " Fortsetzung und Ergänzungen," 1813, iv.,
    col. 1106.
Matthiæ, " Conspectus Historiæ Medicorum chronologicus," 1761,
    pp. 366-7.
Guil. Francois de Bure, " Bibliographie Instructive," 1764 ;
    "Volume . . . des Sciences et Arts," Nos. 1912-1924
    (gives a list of fourteen of his works).
Haller, " Bibliotheca Botanica," 1771, i., p. 425.
Haller, " Bibliotheca Medicinæ Practicæ," 1777, ii., pp. 470, 498.
" Missiv an die Hocherleuchtete Brüderschalt des Ordens des
    Goldenen und Rosenkreutzes," Leszpig, 1783, pp. 61-63.
" Beytrag zur Geschichte der Höhern Chemie," 1785, pp. 520,
    601, 603.
Beckman, " Beyträge zur Geschichte der Erfindungen," 1792, iii.,
    p. 458 ; English translation, 1814, iv., p. 577.
Gmelin, " Geschichte der Chemie," 1797, i., p. 516.
Murr, " Uber den Wahren Ursprung der Rosenkreuzer und des
    Freymaurerordens," 1803, pp. 28, 34, 44, 45, 57.
Fuchs, " Repertorium der Chemischen Litteratur," 1806-8, pp.
    115, 116, 118, 119, 121, 123.
Chalmers, " The General Biographical Dictionary," 1815, xxi.,
    p. 138.
" Biographie Medicale," Paris, Panckoucke (1820-25), vi., p. 236.
" Biographie Universelle," 1820, xxvi., p. 231, n.d. ; xxvi., p. 113
    (article by Weiss, contains a short biography, a list of his
    principal works, and a discussion on the Rosicrucians).
Schmieder, " Geschichte der Alchemie," 1832, p. 353.
"Nouvelle Biographia Generale," 1863, xxxii., col. 862.
Ladrague, " Bibliothèque Ouvaroff, Sciences Secretès," 1870, No.
    1127.
Bauer, " Chemie und Alchymie in Österreich," 1883, p. 18.
H. Peters, "Aus Pharmazeutischer Vorzeit in Bild und Wort,"
    1886, p. 205.
Kopp, " Die Alchemie," 1886, i., p. 220 ; ii., pp. 8, 220, 323, 339, 341,
    350, 354, 366-370, 375, 381, 382, 384.
Bricka, " Dansk Biografisk Lexicon," 1897, xi., p. 67 (art. by S.
    M. Jorgensen).
—*From " Bibliotheca Chemica," Ferguson, ii., pp. 66, 67.*

INTRODUCTION.

THE ordinary vulgar idea that an alchemist was a foolish sort of man, who, greedy of gold and power, spent his strength, his wits, and his money in curious, if not fantastic, experiments, seeking to discover some powder which would, by projection upon lead or inferior metal, transfuse the substance operated upon into gold, and who, in order the longer to pursue this difficult work, sought also for a medicine, the Elixir of Life, has been the common belief of multitudes—one might say the multitude—for ages. It seems that for some time the success of these experiments was believed in—that in effect metals of the baser sort had, by some particularly clever and persevering students of the hidden art, been actually turned into gold. If so, the world has not benefited much thereby, and if the Elixir of Life has been discovered, we have not yet had a complete proof of its action. These beliefs certainly lingered on till, perhaps, the beginning of the eighteenth century, at which time, when the half of that century had passed, they began to be treated with absolute contempt. Those who, rightly or wrongly, had for years—for whole lifetimes—pursued these studies, were thenceforth regarded, not merely with a smile of scorn, but treated as impostors, if not as common swindlers. When the nineteenth century was but in its infancy, other thoughts began to prevail, and some even sought to doubt the truth of the characters, so black and nimious, bestowed upon the old alchemical students. A greater interest began to rise in these quaint, old-world studies. The forgotten works of the students of

Nature began to be read again, and what had begun in curiosity was pursued with a deeper and completer interest.

In the year 1815 was published "The Lives of Alche-mystical Philosophers ; with a Critical Catalogue of Books in Occult Chemistry, and a Selection of the most celebrated Treatises on the Theory and Practice of the Hermetic Art." This useful work has been partly republished, with supplementary items, by Mr A. E. Waite, along with a bibliography, 1888.

In the year 1850, there was issued from the London press of Trelawney Saunders, Charing Cross, a book which may well be described as "epoch making" in the matter before us. "A Suggestive Inquiry into the Hermetic Mystery, with a Dissertation on the more celebrated of the Alchemical Philosophers, being an Attempt towards the Recovery of the Ancient Experiment of Nature." This work, anonymously issued, was subsequently recalled, and only a very few—it is said about twenty-five copies—remain in circulation. It has consequently become in-creasingly rare and valuable. The author, or authors, promise, in a fly-leaf at the end of the work, a further production—"The Enigma of Alchemy and Œdipus Re-solved : A Poem in Five Parts."

The "Inquiry" is said to have been the work of the Rev. T. South, a clergyman of the Church of England, and his sister, and that the withdrawal of the book from circulation was due to the fears of friends that it might cause trouble to the authors. It is, indeed, much to be desired, for the sake of the students of occultism, that the work was republished, with a memoir of the authors, and some account of other manuscripts, which, it is stated, are still in existence, compiled by these accomplished writers. The "Suggestive Inquiry" is a work of the highest class. Its style—pure, cultured, and authoritative—is at once attractive, refined, and shows great mental power, know-ledge of the subjects, and of antiquity. It was a bold venture.

In the year 1857 (second edition, 1865) was published in America a work of this same nature, stated to be the production of General Ethan Allen Hitchcock—" Remarks upon Alchemy and the Alchemists, Indicating a Method of Discovering the True Nature of Hermetic Philosophy, and Showing that the Search after The Philosopher's Stone had not for its Object the Discovery of an Agent for the Transmutation of Metals." This smaller work, though interesting and convincing, is much less ambitious and able than the " Suggestive Inquiry." Its author shows diligence, not learning. It is not the work of a scholar, but of a mind pretty much taken up with one idea.

And the idea of both works is in a measure the same— that the alchemists, under all their labours, their uncouth expressions, and strange, unaccustomed language, hid a deep, solid, and most important secret ; that those who took the trouble to study the subject would find that beneath all was hidden a great moral truth, that Alchemy, like Freemasonry, was a system of morality, veiled in allegory, and illustrated by symbols, and that in the very heart of the alchemical treatises was hidden the greatest moral truth, the greatest moral experiment, which could be conceived ; that man himself was the " Vas," that the training of his moral life was the secret hidden under the stories of the furnace, the crucible, the changing experiments ; that the black state of the " work " represented man as we find him, that the red and white states were representative of his approach to and arrival at the " perfect work " ; all the alchemical processes signified stages on the road to this perfection. When it is asked, Why all this elaborated imagery ? the answer seems not to be so clear. Hints are thrown out that the alchemists were a sort of men who, regarding the official religion of the Middle Ages with semi-contempt, desired to hand on a purer tradition, and for that purpose employed their chemical formulæ. But this is not very satisfactorily established. It is certain enough of most of the alchemists

of whom we have authentic life particulars, that they
did waste time and money in the attempts which they
certainly made for the discovery of material gold. That in
these experiments they made many chemical discoveries is
undoubted. The progress of the world is a warfare, and
they had their part in it. On the other hand, there is
certainly good evidence to show that they had also an
esoteric teaching to give to their more apt pupils. That
from early ages secret colleges and societies existed in
which this teaching was given is, it seems to me, an
incontestible fact, and that many of the so-called sceptics
of Italy, France, and Germany derived their views from
such sources. The Hermetic Science had a secret moral
teaching. It was founded both on Classic story and on
Jewish Kabala. It had roots in Arabian and Saracenic
learning, and had connection with Egyptian hieroglyphics
and Grecian speculation. Opposed with desperate keen-
ness by the Roman Church, in the dome of whose temple
of St Peter, at Rome, runs the legend that St Peter himself
was the " Vas insigne," the deeper and the broader stream
of philosophic thought taught that man, everywhere, in all
religions, was the " Vas insigne," and that by the " work,"
that " Vas " could be made, not merely the instrument, but
the restored and perfected work of Nature—Nature, which
taught even in the flowers, the sweetest and most perfect,
the story of the red and white work in the Rose and the
Lily, or, rather, in the Rose itself, by nature both red and
white.

According to the highest authorities, the Smaragdine
Table of Hermes " comprehends the working principle and
total subject of the art."

It runs thus at the beginning :—" True without error,
certain and most true, that that which is above is as that
which is below, and that that which is below is as that
which is above, for performing the miracles of the One
Thing ; and as all things were from one, so all things arose
from this one thing by adaptation ; the father of it is the

sun, the mother of it is the moon, the wind carried it in its belly ; the nurse thereof is the earth. This is the father of all perfection, a consummation of the whole World."

Human mind is the imperfect Embryo which, by artificial aids, is made conformable to the Divine Wisdom whence it sprang. The eye must be turned away from sensible things, and be fixed for purification on regard to the supreme Intelligible Law within. Man is an epitome of the whole Mundane Creation, and has in him the " germ of a higher faculty," which, when rightly developed and set apart, reveals the hidden Form of Manifested Being, and Secrets of the Casual Fountain, identically within himself. *Causal* Chemia being derived from Cham of Egypt—the blackness of soil—gave origin to the term, the Black Art. Memphis was the city of the art, and there Pythagoras, Thales, Democritus, and Plato were, after being immured in solitude for a year, initiated in all the wisdom of the Egyptians.

The writers of the " Suggestive Inquiry " refer to our author in the highest terms—" But of all those who have connected ancient fable with philosophy, and explained them by the Hermetic Key, Michael Mayer ranks first ; and his works are more esteemed and sought after, even in the present day, than is easily accountable, since he is profoundly guarded in his revelations. Highly curious engravings and woodcuts adorn the works of these authors, and even the title-pages of many of them convey more idea and food for reflection than other modern tomes oftentimes throughout the whole of their development."

The statement of Arnold di Villanova,[1] in his " Speculum," clearly points out that the theory of Alchemy is simple—" That there abides in Nature a certain pure matter, which, being discovered and brought by art to perfection, converts to itself proportionally all imperfect bodies that it touches." [2] " All is in mercury which the wise men seek "—the hidden fire, the *anima*

[1] p. 55. [2] p. 68.

mundi, the mighty Ether, the vehicle of light, the golden
plumage of the Red Lion.

> " The light of life, the vital draught
> That forms the food of every living thing,
> And e'en the high, enthroned, all-sparkling eye
> Of ever mounting fire ; the immense expanse,
> The Viewless Ether, in his general arms
> Clasping the earth, Him call thou Lord and Jove."
> —EURIPIDES.

The " stone " is described by these authors as the " pure
ethereality of Nature, separated by artificial means, purified
and made concrete by constriction and scientific multipli-
cation of its proper light." Nothing is " so closely allied to
the spirit as gold." The dragon, again, is the self-willed
spirit, which is externally derived from Nature by the fall
into generation.[1] Maria Egypta, supposed to be one of the
most ancient hermetic writers, remarks that " the vessel is
a Divine secret, hidden from idolators, and without this
knowledge no one can attain to the magistracy." It is
" the living temple wherein alone the wise of all ages have
been securely able to raise their rejected Stone and Ens of
light." [2]

The question, then, is not so much of outward metals,
but " there is a nearer place yet in which these three,
Mercury, Salt, and Sulphur—Spirit, Body, and Soul—lie
hid together in one place well known, and where they may
with great praise be gotten." These are the words of Basil
Valentine.[3] Morienus has said—" The thing, O King, is
extracted from thee, in the which mineral thou dost even
exist ; with thee it is found, by thee it is received, and
when thou shalt have proved all by the love and delight in
thee, it will increase, and thou shalt know that I have
spoken an enduring truth."

The fall of man assures us that " the wheel of human
life has deviated from its axis into a line which terminates
finally in dissolution, which nothing but their antimonial
spirit, rectified by art, being in bright lines of attraction

[1] pp. 91-94, 113.   [2] p. 138.   [3] p. 142.

and repulsion, as it were a perfect magnet in a star-like circle of irradiated circulation, can contrariate or withstand." [1] The only mystery is *existence*. " Man, then, is the true laboratory of the Hermetic Art ; his life the subject, the grand distillatory and the Thing distilled ; and self-knowledge is at the root of all alchemical tradition." [2] Therefore was it that on the front of the Egyptian temple was inscribed the sentence, " Man should know himself."

> " The path by which to Deity we climb
> Is arduous, rough, ineffable, sublime ;
> And the strong, massy gates through which we pass
> In our first course, are bound with chains of brass ;
> Those men, the first who of Egyptian birth
> Drank the fair water of Nilotic earth,
> Disclosed by actions infinite this road,
> And many paths to God Phœnicians showed.
> This road the Assyrians pointed out to view,
> And this the Lydians and Chaldeans knew."
> —ORACLE OF APOLLO.[3]

This is that Augean stable that was to be cleansed, that most famous labour of the philosophic Hercules, not the least of labours to turn the current of life into another channel, and purify the natural source.

The divine *fire*—" a leaping fire enkindled in the soul— it will nourish itself ; the light beaming from our eyes if directed within, discovers at last that other light which is the substance of its own, until light meeting light, apprehends itself."

The stone of the Apocalypse—that " true crystalline rock without spot or darkness "—this is the midnight sun of Apuleius, the wheel of fire of Ezekiel, the stone with a new name, that pure salt which our Divine Master mentions. It is the "supernatural centre of every living thing." [4] Fire " is the purest and most worthy of all elements, and its substance the finest of all ; for this was first of all elevated in the Creation with the Throne of Divine Majesty." By that Divine infusion man becomes the microcosm. No eye can penetrate that fire which is in

[1] p. 147.   [2] p. 153.   [3] p. 171.   [4] p. 218.

the circumference of the Divinity, it is so intense. This is the " Divine Gloom " described by Dionysius. At present the fire within us is hidden, as the fire in the fuel un-kindled, as gold in the ore unseen. Then the souls of the initiated being made perfect, come, after an orderly passage through the progression of intelligible causes, to a contem-plation of their Highest Unity. Now they desire alone consummation with the Absolute.[1] The " discovery is this —to meet with Him, to be united to Him, and to see Him Himself, the alone with the alone. The Soul hastily with-draws itself from every other energy to Him." This is " more ineffable than all Silence "—Light meeting Light.[2] Paracelsus says that the " true medicine is bound up in man, as milk in a nut." Mind is the true separator. The golden bough is seen, but the tree itself is hidden. All the woes of the Iliad are true, there is but one race, one conflict—the war of Life. A second Achilles appears ; the Son of Man ascends. Böehme says truly—" By death and contrition of the agent in the patient, and *vice versa*, the old life is finally crucified, and out of that crucifixion, by re-union of the principles under another law, the new life is elected ; which life is a very real and pure quintessence, the Mercury so much sought after, even the Elixir of Life, which needs only the corroborative virtue of the Divine Light which it draws, in order to become the Living Gold of the philosophers, transmuting and multiplicating the concrete form of that which in the dead metal we esteem."

" Deus cum solus fuisset in principio, creavit unam substantiam, hanc primam materiam nominamus." The epic circle of Hesiod is said by the Platonists to include the true philosophic secret of the Creation. The Philosopher's Stone is " Ruach Elohim," which " moved upon the face of the waters, the firmament being in the midst, conceived and made bodily, truly, and sensibly in the virgin womb of the greater world, viz., that Earth which is without form." The whole of the Odyssey is an allegory, pregnant with

[1] p. 241.   [2] p. 243.

latent meaning and the recondite wisdom of antiquity.[1] This is the opinion of Maier. The Enigma of the Sphinx means, " in other words, to penetrate rationally the darkened essence of man's own understanding." [2]

The Genesis description of Creation in Nature must be applied to the soul of man, " and " then " there was light." [3] What in physico-chemistry is called " fermentation," is the union of man reduced to the simplicity of the monad with God. This is the whole " work," the reduction of two natures into one. This is immortality consummated. " This is the work, this is the Hermetic method and its end. The line returns to form a circle into its beginning, and they join, not in Time, for their union is in Eternity. This, reader, is the true Christian Philosopher's Stone, which, if it be a chimera, then is the Universe itself not stable, of which it has been proved to be the most exact epitome, having passed the test of experimental reason not only, but analyzed to the last extremity of contrite conscience, is confirmed in operation, visibility, and luminous increase, when rising in rational supremacy over sense and finite reflection the Ethereal Hypostasis revolves in its First Cause." [4] Life is the nucleus of the whole Hermetic Mystery, and the key thereof is Intellect. Man is the proper laboratory of the whole art, the most perfect chemical apparatus. The ancient adepts " discovered the life of man therein circulated to be a pure fire, incorporated in a certain incombustible ethereal vapour . . . and this is the greatest mystery, that man should not only be able to find the Divine Nature but to *effect it.*" [5]

General Hitchcock, in language perhaps plainer, tells us the same story. " This stone is the true *Aurum potabile,* the true quintessence which we seek." [6] Love is the Divine Nature, the Divine Stone, the white stone with the name written on it—God Himself. Love is the philosophic gold. Through this symbolic language the learned then

[1] p. 440.   [2] p. 454.   [3] p. 467.   [4] p. 512.   [5] p. 516.
[6] " Remarks," p. 78.

communicated with each other all over Europe.[1] The
" Roman de la Rose " is itself the most complete specimen
of philosophy extant. " The Rose " is the symbol of the
philosophic gold.

" Three kinds of most beautiful flowers are to be sought,
and may be found in the garden of the wise—damask-
coloured Violets [Love], the milk-white Lily [Purity], and
the immortal Amaranthus [Immortality]. Not far from
the fountain at the entrance, fresh violets do first salute
thee, which being watered by streams from the great
golden river, put on the most delicate colour of the dark
sapphire; the sun will give thee signs. Thou must not
sever such precious flowers from their root until thou
makest the stone, for the fresh ones cropped off have more
juice and tincture, and then pick them carefully with a
gentle and discreet hand; if fates frown not, they will
easily follow, and one flower being plucked, the other
golden one will not be wanting. Let the Lily and the
Amaranthe succeed with greater care and labour." [2]

" A Three-headed Dragon keeps the Golden Fleece.
The first head proceedeth from the water, the second from
the earth, the third from the air. It is necessary that
these three heads do end in One most Potent, which shall
devour all the other Dragons; then a way is laid open to
thee to the Golden Fleece." [3] The " open way to the shut
palace of the King " is " an open way to the knowledge of
God."

Thus " hermetic philosophy does not waste its strength
upon insoluble problems as to the origin or the destiny of
man, but taking *man as he is*, seizes upon the heart and
conscience, and, burying itself there, it lives altogether in
the effort to purify and perfect this source of the issues of
life." [4]

In his recent work, " The Hidden Church of the Holy
Grail," [5] Mr Waite has explained shortly the rise and
meanings of the alchemical work. "Alchemy may not

[1] pp. 149-151.　　[2] p. 159.　　[3] p. 171.　　[4] p. 213.　　[5] p. 533, *et seq.*

have originated much further east than Alexandria, or alternatively, it may have travelled from China when the port of Byzantium was opened to the commerce of the world. In either case, its first development, in the forms with which we are acquainted, is connected with the name of Byzantium." The records of these alchemists penetrated to Arabia and Syria. Then rose a cycle of Latin alchemy. Expositors have interpreted it as merely a process of transmutation of metals, " while others have interpreted it as a veiled method of delineating the secrets of the soul on its way through the world within." There are " schools, experimental, existing in Europe, which claim to possess the master key of the spiritual work." " The name of this correspondence is the Holy Eucharist." Maier was not unaware of this, and I shall give subsequently an account of his hint on this mysterious and awful subject. " The same exalted mystery which lies behind the symbols of Bread and Wine, behind the undeclared priesthood which is according to the Order of Melchisedech, was expressed by the Alchemists under the guise of transmutation." [1]   Here, too, in the elements we have the mystic red and white. " The higher understanding of the Eucharist and the mystic side of alchemy are concerned with the same subject, that is to say, with man, his conversion and transfiguration." [2]   " Christ is therefore the stone, and the stone in adept humanity is the union realized, while the Great Secret is that Christ must be manifested within." [3]

Henry Khunrath was perhaps the first who more elaborately disclosed the under secret of the alchemic mystery. Khunrath was a native of Saxony, born about 1560, and in 1588 received the degree of doctor of medicine at Basle. He practised at Hamburg, and afterwards at Dresden, where he died, 9th Sept. 1605. He published a number of works, now all rare. At Prague, in 1592, " Observationes Zebelis regis et sapientis Arabum Vetustissimi "—a work on astronomy and astrology ; a treatise

---

[1] p. 541.   [2] p. 547.   [3] p. 548.

on " Magnesia Catholica Philosophorum," issued from
Strasburg, 1608 ; but he is chiefly remembered by his
"Amphitheatrum sapientiæ æternæ solius veræ, Christiano-
Kabalisticum, divino-magicum," Hanoviæ, 1609, in folio.
Numerous earlier and other editions are reported, but they
have been considered fictitious. In the edition of 1609,
there is a preface and conclusion by a friend of the author,
Erasmus Wohlfarht.[1]

This work is exceedingly curious, the plates being
mystical and recondite, but have not the beauty, finish, nor
strength exhibited by those in Maier's works. The figures
are accompanied by an introduction showing them to be
illustrative of the universal and particular knowledge of
Nature given in the books of Holy Scripture, the greater
and the lesser world, and in theosophy and kabala. The
plates illustrate the secret and mystery of the Philosopher's
Stone. It is entirely moral and religious. Experience,
reason, the labours of wise men, Nature, the machine of
God ; mind, the spark of the immortal Divinity—all lead
onward to the discovery and possession of " the Stone."
The Christian religion, the Holy Sacraments, and other
unfathomable mysteries, lead upward. One plate shows
how the world of Nature is the mother, but more the
teacher, of the great school in which is to be learned what
the " Lapis " really is. The divine wisdom can only be
attained by labour, prayer, devout meditation. Diligence
is displayed in this figure as absolutely necessary for the
accomplishment of the work. Diligence in common daily
labour would seem to attain this.

The " Lapis " is " Ruach Elohim," that Spirit which
brooded on the chaotic waters, the internal power, form and
genetrix of all things. This is the " Vapor Virtutis Dei."
Chaos, vile, deformed, helpless, is vivified by the working of
the physico-chemical art ; so in man's being, the salt of

---

[1] See as to Khunrath, Ferguson's " Bibliotheca Chemica," i. 462, *et
seq.*, where lists of references and works are given ; article, " Biographie
Universelle," 1818, xxii. 587-8, " Lives of Alch. Writers," Waite, 159, &c.

divine wisdom, the most ancient of "stones" is of universal virtue, and without it and the power of the mystic sun, all is useless.

The mystery of the stone is revealed in the heart of the true lover of wisdom. What, then, is the Ruach Elohim which broods upon the waters? The spirit, the passage, the breath of the Holy, the holy, the flame, the warmth of the power of God—omnipotent, the emanation, the vital fœcundity, the first and highest, the mover, vivicator, issuing from the deepest recess of the Divine; the word by which all things have been produced, clothing earth and water; the first of all material. Yet the Ruach Elohim is the form, the internal and essential form, of all things—the soul of the universal world—" Anima Catholica Multiformis." " Meditate, therefore," says the Theosophist, " and study theosophically to reduce the Ternary by the Quaternary, through the rejection of the Binary, to the simplicity of the Monad, that thy body and soul be gathered to rest in the name of Jesus." " Lastly, after the ashy colour, and the white and the yellow, thou shalt behold the Stone of Philosophers, our King and Lord of Hosts, go forth from the chamber of his glassy sepulchre, into this mundane sphere, in his glorified body, regenerate and in perfection perfected; as a shining carbuncle, most temperate in splendour, and whose parts, most subtile and most pure, are inseparately bound together in the harmonious rest of union into one."

It appears to me that the difference between Maier and Khunrath consists in this:—Maier places the material alchemy first; Khunrath places the spiritual alchemy first. That the latter also claimed to have procured the material medicine seems evident from the following:—" I have travelled much, and visited those esteemed to know somewhat by experience, and not in vain, amongst whom, I call God to witness, I got of one the universal Tincture, and the blood of the Lion, which is the gold of philosophers—I have seen it, touched it, tasted it, smelt it, and used it efficaciously towards my poor neighbours in most desperate cases. Oh! how wonderful is God in His works."

That Maier realised the depth of the spiritual teaching concealed under the alchemical figures is pretty evident from various passages in his works, and this is perhaps most noticeable in the later books.

Hercules is to Maier not merely typified by Samson, but by the Divine Master Himself, in his battle with Cerberus, the king of the powers of darkness. Has not the "chair of St Peter at Rome" represented on it the "labours of Hercules and the signs of the Zodiac"? Does not the "mystery of the seven stars" in the Apocalypse of St John the Divine have reference to the seven planets with their supposed ineffable gifts of wisdom, understanding, counsel, ghostly strength, knowledge, true godliness, and holy fear? The number and the character of the labours of the "twelve apostles of the Lamb," the revelation of God in the Temple, whose floor is of pure gold, its gates pearls, and its foundation precious stones, are typified by the labours of Hercules duly grouped. The twelve signs of the Zodiac were identified with the twelve tribes of Israel. "The twelve tribes were considered by the old theologians to prefigure the twelve apostles, who were said to be analogous to the signs of the Zodiac. In the first century the sun had passed from the Ram to the sign of the Fishes."[1] Thus St Peter the fisherman stands at the head of the twelve.

The red and white ornaments of the girdle of the Amazonian Queen taken by Hercules "have reference to medicines a thousand times more precious than gold."

We Christians, adds Maier at the conclusion of the "Arcana Arcanissima," have revealed to us what was hidden in these old allegorical stories. We have been brought into the full splendour of the true light. Our God has brought us the medicine for both soul and body, truly precious and golden, once by Trismegistus, and now by our "medicus," Jesus Christ, who is the stone cut without

[1] "Canon of All Arts," p. 102.

hands from the highest of mountains, and the corner-stone rejected indeed by the nations, but placed as the cope-stone —the head and glory of the Eternal Temple not made with hands, eternal in the heavens.

In his "Symbola Aureæ Mensæ," Maier refers to the knowledge of the Holy Trinity as revealed by Hermes Trismegistus, and he himself was the creator of all. Moses, he tells us, knew the art, else how could he have dissolved the fragments of the golden calf in the water, and made the Israelites drink them?

But Morien was the first of Christian adepts. Thomas Aquinas has fathomed the truth of the work, for he declares that "in the true Hermetic operation there is but one Vas, one substance, one way, one only operation."

In the seventh triad of his "Phœnix," Maier clearly reveals this secret. "Its deepest secrets," he says, "gave a lively image of our Creation and Redemption. . . Three rivers watered Eden, so three streams water our work. . . All Adam's posterity being subjected to death, the Creator in mercy remembered him, and resolved to save all the human race from death by the greatest of all mysteries. He became Man, born of a Virgin, shedding his Blood, died on the Cross, crushing the head of the Dragon, taking away his poison." Lullius in figures also displays this mystery. The pure comes to the help of the impure, and strengthens the metallic sulphur. "He who sees how Jesus Christ saved us from death, will understand the art, purification, and colour of metals. . . The fixed bodies will never unite with the volatile, unless there is a sweet bond to bring extremes together — "a mediator must be found."

The eleventh guest at Maier's symposium is Melchior Cibinensis, the Hungarian. As a priest dedicated to the ministry of God, he considered himself exempted from serving in the wars against the Turk. As it was for Moses to pursue the war against the enemies of Jehovah, so it was Aaron's place to raise his hands to God. Duly admitted into the order of priesthood, Melchior understood the hidden mysteries of the hidden science, under the sacred form of the Mass. In this service this learned man saw the true mystery of the Philosopher's Stone. In the sacred nativity and life suffering the fire ; then the black and murky death ; and thence the resurrection and life in a ruddy and most perfect colour ; and he made this comparison with the work of the salvation of men, that is, Christ in his natural life, passion, death, and resurrection, which are all commemorated in the divine service of the altar.

"Aperi ergo oculos tuos et vide." There is nothing on earth equal to this celestial work. The whole of the Christian faith is contained here. Thus is the true stone born into the light. Like the Phœnix, by a resurrection a new life is bestowed.

In the most sacred mysteries of the Consecration of the Body and Blood of Christ in the Sacrament of the Altar are hidden the highest and also the deepest secrets of spiritual alchemy.

From the time of Melchizedek, properly designated the priest not of Jehovah, but of the " most high God," we have the first intimation of this mystery, " He brought forth bread and wine "—the first time bread is mentioned in the sacred books.

And the Jews were not ignorant of this sublime secret, for the Tabernacle and the Temple of Solomon were not without its symbols—in the cakes placed on the table of shewbread, and in the wine offering made at certain times. Insomuch was this the case, that for its better observation, " in the captivity of Babylon a postcœnium was instituted by the Jews, with bread and wine for a thanksgiving and a memorial of their going out of Egypt, while being out of the land of promise they could not eat the Pascal Lamb, in imitation of which Christ instituted the Eucharist, to give thanks to God for the general deliverance of mankind,

and in memory of Himself, who was the author thereof, by
the sprinkling of His blood." [1]

"The Eucharistic Bread signifies the super-substantial
sustenance, and the Wine is arch-natural life. It is for this
reason that the Alchemical Stone at the red has a higher
tingeing and transmuting power than the stone at the
white. The first matters of the alchemical work, to make
use of another language of subterfuge, are sulphur, mercury,
and salt; but these are the elements of the Philosophers,
and not those of the ordinary kind. In other words,
common sulphur and mercury correspond to the Bread and
Wine before Consecration, and the philosophical elements
are those which have been transubstantiated by the power
of the secret words. That which is produced is called
Panis Vivus et Vitalis, and Vinum Mirabile, instead of the
daily meat and drink by which we ask to be sustained in
the Lord's Prayer. The Salt is that which is called the
formula of Consecration; it is that which salts and trans-
mutes the natural earth. . . It follows from these
elucidations that the higher understanding of the Eucharist
and the mystic side of alchemy are concerned with the
same subject, that is to say, with Man, his conversion and
transfiguration." [2]

The sublime truth thus taught is that all Christian
mysticism comes out of the Eucharistic service book, and
the divineness of that service came out of the Sacred
Heart. Christ is the Stone, and it is in the perfect service
of the Most Holy Eucharist that the true transmutation
takes place, that the union with Humanity is realised, and
the true secret emerges. This is indeed "Mysterium Fidei."
The "Great Experiment" wrought in the Eucharistic Consecration is from that conveyed in power to, and then
wrought out in, the hearts and lives of the obedient
disciples. Thus is it that "the exalted mystery which lies
behind the symbols of Bread and Wine, behind the un-

---

[1] Sarpi, "Hist. of Council of Trent," Brent, 1676, p. 336.
[2] Waite's "Hidden Church," pp. 545-6.

declared priesthood which is according to the Order of
Melchizedek, was expressed by the alchemists under the
guise of transmutation." Thus Melchior, like his namesake
of olden time, is one of the wisest of men. He it is who
sees, amid all the turmoils of war and tumults of contend-
ing parties and sects, the highest truth revealed to man—
the fact that the alchemist himself is finally the stone.
The natural man, enclosed in the " Vas," as the metal is
enclosed in the vessel, becomes changed into a new life, so
that eventually God abides in man, "for then we spiritually
eat the Flesh of Christ, and drink His Blood, then we
dwell in Christ, and Christ in us ; we are one with Christ,
and Christ with us."

" In this stone there lieth hidden whatsoever God, and
the Eternity, also Heaven, the Starres, and Elements con-
taine, and are able to do ; there never was from Eternity
any thing better or more precious than this .   .   .   he
giveth us his body and blood to eate and to drinke, which
the inward man borne of God receiveth, for the Body of
Christ is every where present in substance ; it conteineth
the second Principle, that is the Angelicall World, according
to which God is called Mercifull, and the Eternall Good.
.   .   For this is the Jewel—the noble Stone. The Diety
brought the flesh and blood together with the Eternall
Tincture in which the soul liveth (viz., the Eternall Fire,
which reacheth into the Diety after the substance of the
majesty, and allayeth, filleth, and strengtheneth itselfe
thereunto), and of Mary in the Virgin into the Holy
Ternary, into which the Word gave itselfe (as a life in the
Tincture of the Eternity), and became the spirit, life, and
vertue of that flesh which sprouteth out of the Tincture of
that fire of the Soule .   .   .   so also in such a manner as
this hath Christ, the true Sonne of God, our Brother, given
to his Disciples his body to eate, and his blood to drink." [1]

---

[1] Sparrow's " Behmen : Three-fold Life of Man," 207-11.

ARCANA ARCANISSIMA hoc est Hieroglyphica Ægyptio-Græca, vulgo necdum cognita, ad demonstrandam falsorum apud antiquos deorum, dearum, heroum, animantium et institutorum pro sacris receptorum, originem, ex uno Ægyptiorum artificio, quod aureu animi et Corporis medicamentum peregit, deductam, Unde tot poëtarum allegoriæ, scriptorum narrationes fabulosæ et per totam Encyclopædiam errores sparsi clarissima veritatis luce manifestantur, suæq tribui singula restituuntur, sex libris exposita Authore Michaele Maiero Comite Palatii Cæsarei, Equite exemto, Phil. et Med. Doct., &c., Cæsar. Mai. quondam Aulico.

The title is surrounded by cuts labelled—Osiris, Typhon, Isis, Hercules, Dionysus, Ibis, Apis, Cynocephalus, and two pyramids, on which hieroglyphics are displayed. No date or place of printing. 4to. Dedication to Paddy on an entablature, p. 1. Dedication to readers, &c., pp. 8. Work itself, pp. 285. Index not numbered, 14 pp. My copy, in gilt edges, has binding in vellum, with floriated cross in centre of both boards, and four open roses at corners, all in gilt. There appears to have been two issues, with different engraved titles. One has an additional leaf preceding the preface. Copies of both, British Museum.

—AUTHOR'S LIBRARY.

The treatise is divided into six books :—

1. Treats of the Egyptian Gods, Hieroglyphics, Osiris, Isis, Mercury, Vulcan, Typhon, &c. ; the Works and Monuments of Kings.

2. Concerning the Grecian Myths, the Golden Fleece and Jason, the Apples of the Hesperides, which all have reference to the Golden Medicine.

3. Genealogies of the fictitious Gods and Goddesses shown to be really philosophic, chemical, and medicinary.
4. Concerning the ancient Festivals and Plays, in which the charm of science was commenced.
5. Concerning the Labours of Hercules and their meanings.
6. Concerning the Trojan Expedition.

The "Arcana" is dedicated to Sir William Paddy, Doctor of Medicine, and President of the London College of Physicians, the patron and friend of the author.

The "Arcana" was the first work published by Maier, and although no date appears on the title, it is believed to have been issued anno 1614, and printed at Oppenheim. The author of the "Alchemystical Writers" says London,[1] but the best authorities give Oppenheim.

Prefixed to the preface is a "Hexasticon a Momo et Mimo distinguens."

In his preface, the author, after referring to the false worships of old ascribed to the gods, and the abhorrence in which such cults are to be held by Christians, who have been taught the truth by the key-word of God, inquires whether these old stories may not have some other meaning, a meaning more secret and arcane. He desires a more original, a deeper, a truer meaning to be found in the old hieroglyphics and stories of these gods and dæmons. The stories of Homer and Heroditus among the Greeks, and those of Livy and Virgil among the Latins, together with the poetic fables, may have other meanings more concealed, and the books of Jamblicus and others have an explanation, which under these stories may unfold to us greater and more wonderful things. Egypt, the most ancient of all, full of the most precious things of God, though its history may now in a measure be involved in darkness, yet to the acute mind may shed a light upon antiquity, and form a sort of grammar which may teach men how to read and explain many interesting things.

These old allegories, stories, and adventures of the gods

[1] p. 292.

may be properly understood as referring to scientific, philosophic, and chemical secrets ; their labours and researches into the powers of Nature, and even their wars and quarrels, may have reference to the labours, the strifes, and the convulsions in Nature and natural substance, for the evolution of new births. Then the stories of Prometheus, Pallas, and Vulcan may be regarded as containing lessons, if not secrets, which may still be interesting, if not actually beneficial, to mankind. There is undoubtedly in the world "Arcana Arcanissima," which, known only to the few, and understood only by a very small number of men, appear to others either like Momus or Mimus, monkey tricks or frightful monsters, but to the wise have true though deeper meanings.

Maier, after making a solemn declaration, " In Christo Spes illa Deo mea amo Cruciatum," concludes with some epigrammatic lines :—

> " Non sedeo tepidus,
> Non sedeo tepidus, Fervere est Christicolarum
> Non frigere animis, neve tepere suis.
> Bis genita æquævi Proles veneranda Parentis
> Ore quia est tepidos evomitura suo."

> M. M. B. G. T. P.

The first book is " De Hieroglyphicis Egyptiorum." Diodorus Siculus has an old story that in the Thebaid, after the inundation of the Nile ceased, a multitude of mice were bred, the precursors of the human race. No trace remains of the most ancient kings, but from the earliest times we find traces of the worship of the sun and moon, Osiris and Isis. In these distant ages the science of the arcanic properties of Nature was taught, and the golden medicine—a thousandfold more precious than the ore ; and philosophic kings and priests knew this secret, hidden under the hieroglyphics of animals, which was the reason and the cause of these animals being held sacred.

Under the types of sun, moon, air, water, earth, the golden medicine was concealed. Masculine Osiris the sun ;

D

feminine Isis, the moon ; Mercury, and Typhon the malig-
nant spirit, were also known and dreaded ; Vulcan-fire and
Pallas, son of Thetis ; the Nile, the water-land, mother of
all. From these gods, celestial and eternal, others were
produced who were in a measure mortal. The first, who
reigned as sovereign, was Saturn ; Dionysus and Ceres
were equivalents of Osiris and Isis.

The golden temple was dedicated to Ammon. Vulcan
and Mercury were greatly respected by the Egyptians for
their invention of things most useful in human life. The
use of fire—its value, its powers, were personified by
Vulcan ; Cain and Abel and Tubalcain, in the ancient
stories, knew its powers. Mercury, again, taught men
rhetoric, astronomy, geometry, arithmetic, and music.
Mercury is Hermes—the oil which softens the hardest
substance. Vulcan and Mercury are more subterranean,
that is " chemici." Osiris has two sons—Anubis the dog,
Macedon the wolf. The story of the adventures of Osiris
shows really the solution of the great work, first to the
Ethiopians—the *Black* Sea, after to the *Red* Sea ; and the
Story of the Poppy is both necessary and arcane. At death,
caused by Typhon, Osiris is divided into twenty-six parts.

Osiris' expedition was really in search of material for
the Golden Medicine—his scattered fragments, collected
by Isis and united, showing the completion of the work.

Observe the nature of Typhon. He is a spirit, fiery
and furious. Isis and Osiris—brother and sister—are
androgyne. Bulls were offered in memory of Osiris. The
pudenda were not recovered. This refers to what remains
after the completion of the great work. It is " nigra et
inutilis."

Two columns were erected to the glory of God and in
memory of Isis and Osiris. The inscriptions are well known.[1]

---

[1] Diodorus, in his work on the Egyptians (*lib.* 1), says that Isis has
deserved immortality, for all nations of the earth bear witness to the
powers of this goddess to cure diseases by her influence. " This is
proved," he says, " not by fable, as among the Greeks, but by authentic
facts." Galen mentions a universal medicine, which in his time was
called Isis.—*Isis Unveiled*, p. 553.

The secrets of chemical knowledge were kept by the Egyptian priests, who seem to have paid more attention to their own interests than those of their countrymen. This priesthood was by succession from father to son, and the knowledge which they communicated to the learned of other nations was brought to Greece by Orpheus and others.

Menes was the great king who gave Egypt laws. Busiris built Thebes. He was a philosopher and priest to Vulcan. The ancient statues and war stories of the Egyptians are allegorical.

A labyrinth was constructed by Miris, similar to that in Greece. Apis the Sacred Bull, distinguished by a white lunar crescent, was sacred to Osiris. The ancient gods of Egypt were few in number, but were expressed by figures of animals, so that in time these animals became recognised as themselves divine. Those figures under which victories in war were obtained were reckoned most sacred. Anubis was the keeper of the parts of Osiris. Great secrets were believed to exist, expressed to the illuminated under these animal figures, but they always acknowledged God as the Creator of all. There were four " chemical gods "—Osiris, Isis, Mercury, and Vulcan.

The black work hidden under the figure of Apis—a black bull. Different cities had different animal cults. The Eagle—signifying the white work. These and the others really meant arcane " physic." The Crocodile, too, venerated at Crocodilopolis—the only four-footed animal that lays eggs—reference here also to the white work. The Ibis, Cat, and Serpent were sacred to Isis and Mercury. The Eagle, one of the most famous of the figures. Ovid, in the " Song of the Pierides," refers to these tales :—

" She sings from earth's dark womb how Typhon rose,
And struck with mortal fear his heavenly foes :
How the gods fled to Egypt's slimy soil,
And hid their heads beneath the Banks of Nile ;
How Typhon, from the conquer'd skies, pursued
Their routed godheads to the seven-mouth'd flood ;
Forced every god, his fury to escape,

> Some beastly form to take, or earthly shape.
> Jove (so she sung) was chang'd into a ram,
> From whence the horns of Libyan Ammon came ;
> Bacchus a goat, Apollo was a crow ;
> Phœbe a cat, the wife of Jove a cow,
> Whose hue was whiter than the falling snow ;
> Mercury to a nasty Ibis turned ;
> The change obscene, afraid of Typhon, mourned ;
> While Venus from a fish protection craves,
> And once more plunges in her native waves." [1]

Then Babylon was an Egyptian colony. Belus was
Jupiter or Saturn. As to the Jews, the circumcision of
boys was practised in Egypt, but whether originated there,
or was brought thither by the Jewish nation, is uncertain.
Athens derived the mysteries of Eleusis from Egypt.
Cadmus, coming from Thebes, wrecked on Rhodes—then
devastated by serpents—is an arcane story referring to the
whole chemical art ? Who does not know the story of the
sowing of the dragon's teeth ? In short, all arts, religion,
and laws came from Egypt. The seven liberal arts were
inscribed on the pillars of Mercury. As to the Pyramids,
they were wrought "ex lapide duro et difficile." The temple
of Bel at Babylon was decorated with lions and serpents
—the solid and volatile, and had a golden table. The
Egyptian art was transferred to the temple at Babylon.
There were both a stone and a golden sceptre, as Jupiter
and Juno were spouses, but also brother and sister—the
sun and moon. The famous draught Nepenthes was made
in Egypt. The statue of Venus at Memphis was made of
gold, and in the sacred rites the adolescent hair of boys
was offered in golden vessels to the magi.

The golden medicine for the cure of ailments of body
and soul was referred to under all these figures. The
medicine known to both Egyptians and Greeks was held to
be comparable to the greatest riches, and is referred to in
all antiquity, even onwards past the time of the Emperor
Diocletian. Gold, the most noble of all substances, became
the vehicle through which not only the greatness of rank

[1] "Metam.," v.

was exhibited, but which, too, rightly understood, became the instrument showing forth the Divine glory, in the preservation of the human body in its greatest strength and power, and amid the frailty and shortness of human life, to those who obey the commandments of God, a source of protection from disease, a help in necessity, and a way by which, living still on earth, man was enriched and sustained. " Idcirco hæc ars a nobis appellata Medicina, quæ aureum animi et corporis Medicamentum perfecit."

The second book of the "Arcana" treats of the symbols of the Greeks, and the stories of the gods in which the golden legends are found.

Vulcan and Mercury, Osiris and Isis—these four became eight, and then twelve. These twelve gods were transferred to Greece, with the Osiraic mysteries, which are those of Dionysus ; while those of Isis are equivalent to those of Ceres. This took place in the time of King Psammitichus, and was done by Orpheus. Their teaching followed as matters of course. Below all the stories of the gods lay an arcane meaning. The supposed murders, sins, adulteries of these gods were really allegories. These were symbols for the eyes, but had a very different meaning when addressed to the heart. Belief in the one God was really, though perhaps secretly, professed. Orpheus sang :—

> " Omnia sunt unam, sint plurimina nomina quamvis.
> Pluto, Persephone, Ceres et Venus alma, et Amores,
> Tritones, Nereus, Tethys, Neptunus et ipse
> Mercurius, Iuno, Vulcanus, Iupiter et Pan,
> Diana et Phœbus jaculator, *sunt Deus unus.*"

The history of Jason's search for the Golden Fleece comes first. He was in possession of the soporific medicine which he gave to the dragon, and was himself carefully anointed to avoid the danger. The story is arcane, and shows the chymic art of gold-making, and, as Natalis informs us, the Philosopher's Stone was really the object of the search. The story is but an allegory. Even boys,

not to speak of men, would never believe these tales about
bulls vomiting fire, &c. Jason represents the medical art,
and it is to be noticed that Medea was born of the sun and
the sea. The ship - Argo—represents the element of fire,
and the Fleece itself the Philosopher's Stone—the chief,
the great medicine of humanity. Virgil refers to the
allegory :—

> " No bulls, whose nostrils breathe a living flame,
> Have turned our turf ; no teeth of serpents here
> Were sown, an armed host and iron crop to bear."

The second allegory is that of the Golden Apples of the
Hesperides :—

> " High rising Atlas, next the falling sun
> Long tracts of Æthiopian climates run ;
> There a Massylian Priestess 1 have found,
> Honour'd for aye, for Magick Arts renowned.
> Th' Hesperian Temple was her trusted care ;
> 'Twas she supplied the wakeful dragon's fare ;
> The poppy-seeds in honey taught to steep ;
> Reclaimed his rage, and soothed him into sleep ;
> She watched the golden fruit."

What was this gold ? those apples of golden colour ? the
garden ? The twelve labours refer to the celestial signs.
Hercules is the labourer, the artificer who from his labours
evolves the golden medicine. What is the dragon ? The
same as Cerberus, the Sphinx, the Chimæra ; the tree,
vegetable life in general. It has its roots sunk in the
ground, grasping the gold beneath.

The temple of Saturn was the treasure-house where the
golden money was guarded. The golden apple thrown by
Eris, the uninvited guest to the marriage of Peleus and
Thetis, with the inscription, " to the fairest," was the
proximate cause of the Trojan war; and then the story of
Hippomenes and Atalanta—the three golden apples so
beautiful that Atalanta could not forbear from picking
them up when she ran in the race, and so was distanced by
Hippomenes. On account of their subsequent conduct,
they were turned into lions—" Hoc est in vase noto seu
in domo vitrea et vertuntur in leones."

" Aprum occidit, quia altera Diana est, Fontem ex saxo elicit prope fanum Æsculapii ; Quia petræ philosophiæ durissimæ dant aquam."

The stag of Ceryneia had golden horns, but brazen feet. Hercules was ordered to bring it alive. He pursued it a whole year, and caught it wounded. The golden sun. Arnold has said, " In one stone are the sun and moon in virtue and power. Two horns—the sun neither without the moon, nor the moon without the sun. The stone is invincible, though its powers and virtue are hidden.

" Philosophi dicunt strenue, duo animalia esse in hac sylva, unum laudabile, formosum et alacre ; magnum et robustum Cervum aliud unicornu, monstrat Philosophus." That thing whose head is red, eyes black, feet white—that is our magisterium. The feet are properly referred to, being " basis est operis."

Bacchus, who is Dionysus and Osiris, the first of the golden gods. is the giver of gifts. Midas is a symbol—golden, making gold.

Other symbols then are—the golden age, the golden shower which fell in the Isle of Rhodes, the golden harvest. The golden age, the Saturnian ; the silver, the Jovian. Then the brass and the iron ages.

" And thou, O Argive Juno, golden shod."

Rhodes—the isle of roses, red-golden—where the shower fell. Vulcan, the " midwife," produces Pallas—the wisdom of Jove. That is " perfecta cognitio rei occultæ." This virgin is perfect and begotten of Jupiter—the golden crown of Pythagoras—melts in golden song.

The third book treats of the genealogy of the gods, the philosophical tree with its innumerable branches—the golden chain.

Homer's golden chain of gods — the strange puzzle whether the egg or the hen first existed—whether the earth or the gods were first in being. Plato, the divine,

and the Christian teachers affirm that the Eternal efficient
Cause existed eternally, and that the world was made at
his will in time. The golden chain of the genealogy of the
gods produces them, " ex cœlo et Terra itaque Saturnus et
Rhea progenti sunt " ; " Cœlum est agens et terra parens."
Saturn was the most ancient of the dieties, the father of the
Golden Age. The colour of Saturn is black, the first state
of the " work." Then he wars with the Titans, " Idcirco et
Saturno amputatas viriles partes dicunt, et cum sal in
aquam tanquam in mare decidat, ex illo sale et sulfure
gignitur Venus." Was not " the stone " vomited up by
Saturn to be seen in Helicon ? Then the symbol of Ætna
in flames—the work proceeding. It is said that Juno, the
daughter of Saturn and Ops, was the sister and wife of
Jupiter. This is nothing else but the water of Mercury,
which is called Juno. The very earth distills Jupiter,
Juno. It is but the vitrous vessel in which is the salt.
In this is concealed the most ancient chemical philosophy,
hidden amongst the Egyptians and Greeks, shewn in relics,
in hieroglyphic pictures, sung by the different poets.

" Jupiter est idem Pluto, Sol et Dionysus." All riches
are in Juno, held in golden chains. The hundred-eyed
peacock, the bird of Juno, refers to the dragon's tail ; and
those Pyrenean mountains, which Pluto inhabits, refer to
the mines wherein the metal is sought by the Phœnicians.
There is a mystic reason why Pluto and Pallas have a
common altar, " Ad Chemarum fluvium rapuit Proser-
pinam." Isis bears horns—referring to Luna. The bees,
symbols of the Muses, showing the flying, volant nature of
the substance. Fire was among the Romans the sacred
symbol, perpetually kept alive by the Vestals.

" Quid est Venus ? Quod homo materiale corpus." Did
not Cadmus, born of the power of the basilisk, sow the
dragon's teeth ? His wife was Harmonia. He was the
founder of Thebes. Fire " id est draco." The Sun is the
eye of the Universe, the King of the Planets. Of it did not
Anáxagoras say that it was a burning red stone ? The

ancients believed that the eclipses were signs of the passions and diseases of the sun or moon. What was held to be the "apex mundi?" The golden altar in the Temple of Delphi. The symbols of birds under which Orpheus and others appear, from their volatile nature refer to the "work."

The story of Æsculapius is well known. The Greeks knew him as Asclepius. He was the descendant of Apollo. A raven (the black work) was associated with his birth. Some say Hermes saved him from the flames. The serpent was his perpetual symbol. The goat and the cock were offered to him. " Si vero dicatur Mercurius extraxisse Æsculapium ex cineribus matris, eodem res redit ; Hoc enim est officium Mercurii et nil nisi Mercurius est, de quo dicitur." This is the sum and head of arcane philosophy and medicine. " Rubedine seu Apolline nato, hic in ipso vase concumbit cum Coronide, seu instar cornicis nigra nympha, et generat Æsculapium, hoc est, omnis medicinæ Philosophicæ authorem." The two serpents twined on the rod represent the male and female, the working, the suffering, the liquid and the dry, the cold and the humid. The " stone" is the result of the junction of these two ; " hæc est duplex facies Jani." The two birds, one with feathers, the other without. Mercury was the producer, the universal ground of the Egyptian religion. Ulysses was initiated in the same Thracian mysteries of the three great gods whom it was turpitude to name—Axioerus, Axiocersa, Axiocersus, " triceps Deus vocatur, marinus, cælestis et terrestris habitus." All these ancient and most arcane teachings " ex Egypto in Phœnicium, et ad Græcos cum sua religione mystica penetravit, ab his ad Romanis "— Mercury in Egypt was called Theut, hence the Germans, who held his cult very strongly, became known as Theutones, or Teutons.

Horace, in his ode, " ad Mæcenatem " (iii. 16), is pressed into service. The birth of Perseus, son of Danaë, preceded by the story of his mother's seclusion, is an arcane story :—

> " Of watchful dogs, an odious ward,
> Might well one helpless virgin guard,
> When in a tower of brass immured,
> And by strong gates of oak secured,
> Although by mortal gallants lewd
> With all their midnight arts pursued,
> Had not great Jove, and Venus fair,
> Laugh'd at her father's fruitless care,
> For well they knew no fort could hold
> Against a god when chang'd to gold."

The story continued tells how Perseus, come to age, cut off the Gorgon's head, then went to Argos and turned his grandfather Acusius into a " stone."

Hermes, or Apollo, gave Amphion a lyre. He and his brother Zethus, having taken possession of Thebes, when Amphion played his lyre, the " stones" not only moved of their own accord to the place where they were wanted, but fitted themselves together so as to form the wall. Hence Horace in "Arte Poetica " :—

> " Thus rose the Theban wall : Amphion's lyre
> And soothing voice the listening stones inspire."

The fourth book—as to the Grecian feasts and sacred times, and the plays celebrated in memory of the philosophic work.

When God, the greatest and the best, chose the Israelites for his people, through Moses he instituted certain recurring festivals, in addition to that of the seventh day, which had been set apart in memory of Jehovah resting from His works in the creation of heaven and earth—the Pascal, the Pentecostal, and the Feast of Tabernacles. Amongst the Greeks, the Romans, and the Egyptians, the same intention was observed. The feasts of Osiris, Ceres, and Adonis and others similar, were of very ancient date. These were all instituted to keep before the eyes of the people the histories of the gods and heroes. The result as the intention was different. The one set of festivals was to show forth the glory of God ; the others, invented by man, served to keep up a series of fabulous stories, such as that of Apis and Dionysus. Not merely so, but the Phallic

COUNT MICHAEL MAIER. 43

rites were used "quibus lignea virilia thyrsis alligantes
gestabant." The Canephoria were celebrated in honour of
Dionysus, in which golden baskets were carried, containing
the first fruits; the Bacchanalia, described by St Augustine;
the death of Orpheus, the celebration of which, an allegory,
had an arcane meaning; the "Festa Cereris." Triptolemus
"sub igne nutritus . . . est noster ille fœtus philosoph-
icus." The salamander, an animal which lives in fire, may
easily point " in operibus chymicis." This opinion is supported from the writings of Avicenna, Lullius, Ripley, and
others. Then there were the Eleusinian Mysteries, to the
consideration of which a considerable part of the chapter is
devoted. The " Somnium Scipionis" is largely referred to.
In all these we have the " stone," the " Dragon," and " Sol
et Luna"; the very names of the planets referring to our
" medicine"—the sun, the image of active power; the
moon, the emblem of passivity; Mercury, " receptaculum
utriusque." This is shown from the Rosary, from Hermes
and Lullius. " They had, Diodorus telleth, a brazen statue
of Saturne, of monstrous bigness, whose hands hang down
to the earth so knit one within another that the children
that were put in them fell into a hole full of fire." " Isis,
which is all one with Ceres." [1] Adonis is the sun. Perhaps
the Lampadephoria are illustrative of our " work." These
games were used in this manner. Runners carried a lamp
or torch from one point to another in a chain of competitors, each of whom formed a successive link. The first,
after running a certain distance, handed the lamp or torch
to the second, and so on till the point proposed was reached.
Heroditus uses the game as a comparison to illustrate the
living image of successive generations of men. " The action
of carrying an unextinguished light from the Cerameicus to
the Acropolis is a lively symbol of the benefit conferred
by the Titan [Prometheus] upon man, when he bore fire
from the habitations of the gods, and bestowed it upon
man." But the gratitude to the giver of fire passed to

[1] L. Vives in Aug. de Civit. Dei, 1610; vii. 19, 20.

Hephaestos, who taught men to apply it to melting and
moulding of metal. Other writers hold that the game had
an inner significance, "alluding to the inward fire by which
Prometheus put life into man." [1] One symbol on a coin
referring to these games shows a serpent surrounding in a
circle. Reference is also made again to the common altar
of Vulcan and Pallas, to the fire of Vesta, to the chief place
which Vulcan held amid the Egyptian gods, and to the
Germanic races.

The Olympic games, the Isthmian and the Nemean
games, all come under notice. The Olympic games were
celebrated according to the ancient mode of reckoning
every four years. It is said on the first full moon after the
summer solstice. The fourth day of the festival was the
day of the full moon. Sacrifices were continually offered
during the time the games were going on. The victor was
crowned upon a bronzed tripod, afterwards upon a table
made of ivory and gold. [2]

The "Pythia" were one of the four great national
Greek festivals. These games were celebrated in honour of
Apollo, and appear at first as a musical competition —lyre-
playing—in honour of the god of song and music. Apollo
is Helios, the sun—the Egyptian Horus. Apollo killed the
dragon Python on Mount Parnassus. He was the father of
Asclepius, the god of the healing art. The lyre and the
bow are the emblems of Apollo. He slew the "dragon"
Typhon. " De putrefactione hujus Typhonis, unde Python
et Pythia nomen acceperunt." The slaying of the "dragon,"
and the use of the putrified black matter is well known in
the "art." Morien—" Hæc terra cum aqua sua putresit et
mundificatur quæ cum mundata fuerit, auxilio dei totum
magisterium dirigetur."

The fifth book, concerning the Labours of Hercules.

The history and the fame of the labours of Hercules are
well known throughout the whole world. They have been

[1] Smith, *in voce.*   [2] Smith, *in voce.*

sung by poets—for who is ignorant of his praises? All nations unite in this, for he was the most celebrated of all the heroes of antiquity. Orpheus " horum primus author est." Hercules was the son of Zeus, by Alcmene of Thebes, in Boeotia. His step-father was Amphitryon. Put to the breast of Hera when an infant, she pushed him away, and the milk thus spilled produced the Milky Way. So strong was he and wise, that in his early childhood he killed two serpents which Hera had sent into his sleeping room. In his labours, successes, and troubles he was typified by Samson among the Israelites, and the Divine Son himself was foreshown by Hercules in his battle with Cerberus and other inhabitants of the infernal regions. This similitude is drawn out to some length by Maier. Hercules, Jason, and Ulysses, in their labours and journeys, have an arcane and chemic reference. Hercules, in his perfection and strength, is an emblem of what is required to " the work."

" Completa organa," a sickly and feeble body is useless. That constancy and perseverance which Hercules showed is an absolute prerequisite. Proficiency in many arts is ascribed to Hercules—poetry, music, astronomy, horsemanship, chariot-driving, archery, fighting in heavy armour.

The first labour was the fight with the Nemean Lion. He stopped up the lion in its den, and strangled it with his own hands. This has a chemic significance. The " lion" is well known in our " work," " ex spuma lunæ natus est." " Leo viridis est vitrum." Many writers—Morienus, Ripley, Senior—the lion the strongest of animals—" leonem est solem, qui habeat lunarem naturam adjunctam."

The second labour was the fight with the Lernean Hydra. Like the lion, this creature was the offspring of Typhon and Echidna. Hercules killed this monster by fire. It had, by its poison, infected the air, causing the death of men and animals. A gigantic Crab came to the assistance of the Hydra, referring to the sign of Cancer in the heavens. Geometry has divided the heavens by twelve signs. " Noster serpens in arte ex aqua concrevit." This is our lizard, serpent, and hydra, which, if not properly killed, will revive again, that is, its life will continue by reason of its volatile nature.

The third labour was in connection with the Stag of Ceryneia, which had golden horns and brazen feet. Hercules wounded or killed it. He pursued it a whole year. This story has been referred to in the second book of the "Arcana." Hercules next attacked the Erymanthean Boar. Chasing him through snow, he caught him in a net and carried him to Mycenæ. When pursuing this labour, he came upon the Centaur, and in its pursuit wounded Cheiron. The fight with the Centaurs gave rise, it is said, to the institution of mysteries. Two mountains come into these stories. " Fili, inquit Calid cap. 10 vade ad montes Indiæ et ad suas cavernas, et accipe ex iis lapides honoratos."

The cleansing of the stables of Augeas. This was to be performed in one day. It was done by letting two rivers flow through. The reward being refused, Augeas and his sons were slain. In memory the Olympian games were instituted by Hercules. Apis is referred to in this tale. The cleansing refers to the purification of the vile material in the philosophic work. " Duo lapides jacent in stercore, unus fœteus, et alius bene odorans." " Merculinus apud Rosar. Est lapis occultus et in imo fonte sepultus, vilis et ejectus simo vel stercore tectus."

The Stymphalian Birds—voracious creatures which fed on human flesh. Raising them with a brazen rattle, Hercules killed them with arrows. Some say that they were afterwards found by the Argonauts. The rattle was the work of Vulcan. It is of these that Apollonius, in the Argonautics, speaks :—

> " When great Alcides on Arcadia's soil
> Pursued the progress of his glorious toil,
> From fair Stymphalus' wide expanse to chase
> The brooding Ploïdes, pernicious race,
> Most foul and hateful of the plumy kind,
> I saw the chief. His quiver he resign'd ;

His station on a lofty rock he took,
His mighty hands the brazen cymbals shook,
Far fled the brood abhorr'd, on sounding wings,
And darken'd air with screams of terror rings."

Naturally viewed, the story is foolish, but viewed philosophically, most beautiful and clear. The birds are the volatile parts of the " work," easily dispelled, " ut et de Crotalo seu ære philosophico, fixo, figenti eas." " Constans in turba dicit, nihil alius curate, nisi quomodo duo sunt argenta viva, scilicet fixum in ære, et volatile fugiens in Mercurio."

The Wild Bull of Crete, which Hercules caught; the Mares of the Thracian Diomedes. These latter Hercules had to fetch to Mycenæ. They were fed on human flesh. " Equus noster leo fortis sub pallio coopertus."

The Girdle of the Amazonian Queen was taken by Hercules, but not till he had killed her. The girdle was adorned with the most precious ornaments, white and red, and has reference to medicines a thousand times more precious than gold.

Then there are the greatly embellished adventures with the Oxen of Geryones, in Erytheia. Geryones was a monster with three bodies, living in the " reddish island," under the rays of the setting sun. " Geryon ille tricorpor, Chrysaoris filius, hos boves habuit." " Geryon quid ? " Hamuel answers, " Est aqua vitæ triplex, quia est unum, in quo sunt, scilicet aër, ignis et aqua, in qua est anima exorta, quam vocant aurum, et vocant eam aquam divinam." In his adventures, Hercules felt so annoyed at the heat, that he shot at Helios, who, admiring his boldness, presented him with a golden cup or boat, in which he sailed over to Erytheia.

The story of the Golden Apples of the Hesperides has been referred to in the second book of the "Arcana."

In all Maier expands the acts, labours, and deeds of Hercules to the number of thirty-six, the fetching of Cerberus from the lower world being the last and the greatest. When Cerberus appeared in the upper world,

unable to bear the light, " he spat, and thus called forth
the poisonous plant called aconitum"—a potent medicine.
Hercules is the picture of perfect philosophic work. He
bears in his history the key to the interpretation and
intelligent understanding. By fire he destroyed the evil.
" Moneo, caveatis, ne compositum fumiget et fugiat." By
his strength, good fortune, and constancy, through perseverance amid the greatest labours, he teaches us in what
way to pursue our studies, that in the most arduous affairs
we may gain the crown from men, and immortality from
God.

    Book sixth—concerning the Trojan Expedition.

    Dictys of Crete, said to have been the companion of
Idomeneus in the Trojan War, writes his experiences. But
the story of the founding of the city is easily seen to be
fabulous, because the alleged founders are themselves
fabulous. Vulcan is said to have built the walls with his
own hands—Vulcan, the god of fire ; and Neptune, the god
of water. Without these elements, no work could be done.
So in the " work," " in medio et in fine." Trees and stones
could not, even at the music of Apollo's lyre, have fixed
them in proper places. The ancient kings of Troy are also
fabulous. But the whole story is well known to everyone.
It need not be repeated. The Trojan names are Greek.
The story of the golden apple thrown by Eris, and which is
said to have been the remote cause of the war, is evidently
a fable. The whole tale is so mixed up with fictitious gods
and heroes as to be impossible of belief. The dates are so
indefinite that nothing can be concluded from them. The
dates given by Homer were evidently taken out of his own
imagination. The Roman story of Romulus is equally
confused, Who will believe that he was born of Venus
and Mars ? and what matter is it that a she-wolf suckled
him ? These foolish stories—" aquila fundavit, anser pro-
texit gallina gubernavit Romam gentilitiam." How could
there be gods of whom the poets make comedies and

dishonour with foul imputations ? King Midas' story is
well known, and has been already referred to. The lust of
gold, the horrible power achieved, the prayer for delivery.
The happy release was gained :—

> " The King instructed to the fount retires,
> But with the golden charm the stream inspires,
> For while this quality the man forsakes,
> An equal power the limpid water takes—
> Informs with veins of gold the neighbouring land,
> And glides along a bed of golden sand "

Six reasons are given why Troy could not be taken.
But it was Discord that really threw the golden apple,
which, she cried, was for the most beautiful. This evil was
then the beginning of all the Trojan misfortunes. The
overthrow of Troy-town is, under the philosophic and
arcane story, the most arcane of all ; and the highest
points—the very " arcanissima "—relate to the great and
noble Achilles, beloved of gods and men. " Hoc sit clavis
totius artis." It can never be, and has never been, expressed
in words by the philosophic workers. This son of Peleus,
by the Nereid Thetis, is educated by Phœnix, and by the
centaur (dragon) Cheiron taught the art of healing. To
make her son immortal, Thetis anoints him with ambrosia
by day, and holds him in the fire at night to destroy his
mortal elements. His father sees him baking in the fire,
makes an outcry, whereupon Thetis returns to the Nereids,
taking the form of a cuttle-fish (the " black work").
" Locus est Magnesia." Pythagoras says—" Et sciendum
quod nihil aliud est hujus artis scientia, quam vapor et
aquæ sublimatio, argenti vivi Magnesiæque corpori con-
juncto." Achilles trained in the fire, " ut vere Pyrisous
et salamandra nostra fiat," is slain at Troy and reduced to
ashes. " Nihil aliud, ab Homero mystice et occulte intel-
lectum est, quam vasis philosophi, in quo Helena et Paris,
materia principalis continetur arcte conclusa, ab igne suo
circumeunte, vaporoso et digerente periodus et ambitio."
From the ashes the Phœnix arises, Æneas, and others, who
build a new city and found new kingdoms. This is the

E

summary and total of Homer's story. Achilles and Pyrrhus "noster laton est, nostra Magnesia, noster ignis." The whole was the " philosophic work," thus determined and explained long ago, in 1548, by Dionysius Zacharius Gallus.

What, then, was the Palladium which was taken from the Trojan citadel ? There have been various opinions as to this. It was afterwards placed in the temple of Vesta, at Rome.

Under all these old stories and hieroglyphics an arcane, hidden meaning lies. But we Christians have revealed to us what was hidden—the benefits and blessings given to the world by God Omnipotent, through whose power these old allegories have been made plain. So to him, the Triune God, with all the devotion of our minds and hearts, we render thanks, who, through His most tender mercy, has delivered us from the idolatry of these ancient nations, delivered us from their darkness and errors, and brought us into the true light, shining in full splendour ; and who has brought to us medicine for both soul and body, being precious and golden, once by Trismegistus, now by our " medicus," Jesus Christ, to whose name be now ascribed all honour, and from whom we may at last receive eternal life, " qui ut Lapis ex alto monte sine manibus revulsus, et lapis angularis a potiori mundi parte seu gentibus rejectus nobis appropriatus, sit benedictus in secula. Amen."

DE CIRCULO PHYSICO, QUADRATO : Hoc est, Auro, ejus que virtute medicinali sub duro cortice instar nuclei latente; an et qualis inde petenda sit, Tractatus haud inutilis : Authore Michaele Majero Com. P. Med. D. Eq. exem. &c.

Vignette—a circle enclosing a square ; inside the circle—Ignis, Terra, Aqua, Aer ; outside the circle—Siccum, Frigidum, Humidum. Calidum. Oppenheimii Typis Hieronymi Galleri, Sumptibus Lucæ Jennis, 1616. Dedicated to Maurice, Landgrave of Hesse, pp. 3, Work, pp. 79, all one pagination. Dedication dated at Frankfurt, "Anno 1616, Mense Augusto." After the dedication on pp. 6, 7, is " Carmen authoris summam libri exponens."

—AUTHOR'S LIBRARY.

There are three joined together in chains of Concord, for the harmony of the world. " Cor humanum, Sol cæli atque Aurea virtus." The sun is king; by its power the human heart beats and gold is produced. The heart rules over the human existence, as the sun rules over the heavens, from it flows the current of life. On the earth, again, gold rules. It is the looking-glass which reflects the riches in the world. God has given us the sun, the sun gold, and these both power to the heart of man. The sun is the image of God, and the heart is the image of the sun, and gold continually shows forth God's honour.

The contents of the twelve chapters follow.

Gold is the image of the absolute circle written upon Nature.

Within the golden circle is a quadrature of four equal parts.

Gold, again, which is the sun of the earth, is the centre

of human action, as well as of the heavenly planets. It is
the most precious of all terrene things, in its outward
beauty, colour, purity, splendour, weight, and innocuous
quality. It is, in its incorruptible and imperishable nature,
an active image of eternity.

But it has also in it a medicinal quality, given for the
aid and comfort of the human race.

The tenth chapter is " De auro æquato, quomodo agat in
non æquata visceræ corporis humani et intemperiem
illorum emendet."

Chapter twelve is "Cantilena Anacreontea." The virtue
of the Hellebore, for which Anticyra was so famous, is far
excelled by that of the medicinal gold. Hercules, in his
madness, was healed with this Anticyran medicine, but the
virtue of the golden medicine far excelled it. Roses and
lilies are sweet and pleasing, but it is only

"Metals that would be gold if they had time."

Nature ever strains after perfection ; and gold being the
most perfect metal, it is evident that Nature's intention is
that, becoming perfect, all metals should become gold.
Metals are distinguished by degrees of maturity. "The
difference between lead and gold is not one of substance,
but of digestion."

LUSIUS SERIUS, Quo Hermes sive Mercurius Rex
Mundanorum omnium sub homine existentium, post
longam disceptationem in Concilio Octovirali habitam,
homine rationali arbitro, judicatus et constitutus est.
Authore Michaele Majero Com. Pal. Med. D.
Horat. Omne tulit punctum, qui miscuit utile dulci.

Cut on title—king on throne, Mercury winged, with Caduceus ;
animals, birds, insects, &c. Oppenheimii Ex Chalcographia Hieronymi Galleri, sumptibus Lucæ Jennis Bibliop. 1619. Dedication,
3 pp.-- " To three sagacious doctors of medicine, expert chemists, and
most jocund friends—Francis Anthony, of London ; Jacobus Mosanus,
and Christianus Rumphius." Dated at Francfurt, "ipso ex Anglia
reditu, Pragam abituriens, anno 1616, Mensi Septembri." 4to, pp.
79. Also editions, 4to, Oppenheimii, L. Jennis, 1616 ; 4to, Frano-
furti, 1617. —Author's Library.

LUSUS SERIUS : or, Serious Passe-time. A Philosophi-
call Discourse concerning the Superiority of Creatures
under Man. Written by Michael Mayerus, M.D.,
London. Printed for Humphrey Moseley, at the
Prince's Arms in S. Paul's Church-yard ; and Tho.
Heath in Convent-garden, neere the Piazza, 1654.

[Size :—] 5⅔ × 3¼ inches. [No. of pages, numbered] 1-139. [The
back of p. 139 is blank, and the two following leaves.] [Dedicated]
To the Honourable, Cary Dillon, Esq., Son to Robert, late Earle of
Roscommon. [Signed at the end] J. de la Salle.
—Bodleian Library.

LUSUS SERIUS : Serious Passe-Time. Wherein Hermes
or Mercury is declared and established King of all
Worldly things, &c.

"After it had been very hotly debated in the great
amphitheatre of the world, to whom of all those that
presented themselves as competitors, the Preheminence and
Soveraignty were most due," there were so many different
opinions, that it was agreed representatives should be
elected, from the four-footed two, and one each from birds,
Fishes, Insects, creeping things, Vegetables, and Minerals,
and sent to the next Parliament, where, before Man, as the
fittest judge, a King should be chosen from these eight.   A
parliament of eight was at last called, that is, the Calf and
Sheep, the Goose, the Oyster, the Bee, the Silk Worm,
Flax, and Mercury, who made each their address to Man,
as he sat, richly arrayed, on a little tufted hillock in the
midst of a flowery ground.

THE CALF.

We are serviceable by our labours, in tilling ground, by
which means corn, wheat, oats, &c., are grown, and hence
bread.   We are still used for drawing wagons in Italy and
in other places.   So useful the Egyptians found us, that
they adored us as deities, and gave us all honours.

By what we yield for use of man, dung and milk.   Our
dung is the food of the fields, which feed man, and are his
joy and recreation.   It also serves man for medicine,
applied outwardly for Gout, Tumours, and Dropsies ;
inwardly for Jaundice and like diseases.   Also used for
fuel.   For milk, there are too many profits to declare all.
Butter, cheese, and whey all made from it.   From what I
have said will be seen we contribute not only bread and
drink, but all things made from milk.

From our carcass, beef, the bravest food ; from our guts
many dishes are made ; our tallow for many excellent
services and pies, and shares empire with the sun by
affording candles.   Our bones and horns, many instruments ; bladders, to keep the air from bottles ; hair for
mortar ; hides for boots, shoes, bellows ; calves-skins made
into drums and books, patents, letters, and other writings ;

hence laws and ordinances, hymns, anthems, libraries, where all records are preserved.

THE SHEEP.

The sheep, the meekest and mildest of creatures, should prove a merciful King. Supplies man with wool, hence clothes man from crown of his head to sole of his foot—his hat, his coat, stockings, all woolen.

Our milk, the fattest and sweetest ; our cheese, a great delicacy. Our dung best for ground. Saltpetre from the effects of our urine, which takes away the effects of gunpowder, and is good for jaundice, scalds, burns, plaisters.

After death, for the palate of man ; our skins, for women's ornaments and parts of men's habits and gowns ; the bare pelt for parchment, rolls for records ; my bowels make musical instrumants and bows ; the Turks make string from our guts.

THE GOOSE.

We can live in earth, air, and water ; but if that is not enough, my quills are used for writings, my eggs are eaten, my dung is used for several disease. My chief use is at Michaelmas, when I make an excellent dish roasted, and my guts and gibblets another dish. My feathers are used for men's beds, where half their life is spent. My quills and feathers used for arrows. 'Twas we once gave the alarm and saved the city of Rome. Where is the use of the calf and sheep-skins without our quills, by whose means Emperors rule and laws made ? All learning by means of pens.

THE OYSTER.

I am born and bred in the noblest element—the vast ocean. Chastity is a peculiar property of our kind, as appears in our not propagating in the common way. By a wonderful process, we make the noblest presents that man can receive, whether in medicine or for delight and ornament, i.e., pearls ; in medicine, they strengthen the heart.

They are prepared into milk, oil, liquor, water, and salt, for medicinal purposes. They assist women in sterility. We are a choice food for man, and also greatly cherish and fill the spermatick vessels of either sex, hence powerful assistants in the generation of men. Shells useful for hilts and handles of instruments, household furniture, &c. As for the " Margarites" themselves, of inexpressible value. Cleopatra had some, valued at 2000 oxen, yet she destroyed one of them at a draught, to outvie Mark-Antony. That which dazzles the world by its value should surely be royal. 'Tis we that adorn queens, princes, nobles, Kings. We make scepters, and adorn royal robes.

THE BEE.

What creatures acknowledge a king, but man and the bee ? For our nobility, we are propagated by a peculiar indulgence and warmth of Heaven ; starting as little worms, after a time ennobled and become bees ; hence not made, but born honourable and ennobled by Nature herself by being made animals. Our chastity, a great commendation to any prince. No creature swifter than we. Alexander the Great and Julius Cæsar, victorious by celerity. Our stings useful to strike enemies, but only when provoked. We offer no injury to man, who robs our hives ; we are easily pacified with tinckling music, and therefore musical creatures like man. Also we sing ourselves perpetually.

Our profits to man, firstly, honey, contributing to length of life and health. Useful in medicine. Secondly, wax, useful for wax-candles, especially in churches, used by Christians and heathens ; wax used medicinally in plaisters, salves, and ointments. Lastly, wax was used by the ancients for communicating of laws, commands, &c.; aud for seals ; what use letters or documents without seals ? Calves and sheepskins, written on by goose-quills, null and void without seals. Also used for wax-images in churches.

Man himself may seem to have learned from us the arts
and secrets of monarchical government.

THE SILK-WORM.

Nobly born ; from a little seed shed by a four-winged
Insect, is produced the silk-worm. These make little silks
threads, reeled and gathered into skeins by man, whose use
is unspeakable. Then dyed all colours. Consider only how
many people employed weaving, dying, weaving into stuffs,
and selling—more people than in any Prince's dominion.
Then how many who have their clothing from us ? The
greatest man of no esteem unless clad in fine clothes.
Consider the story of Philip, Duke of Burgundy, who one
night placed in his own bed a drunken cobbler, and the
next day, dressed in silks and fine cloths, he took the place
of the real duke, and indeed began to think he was the
duke, until being drunk again, he was re-clothed in his
rags, and on waking thought he had dreamt it all. All
which proves the power of silken garments and fine clothes.
Some barbarous nations know not our value, but prefer to
go unclothed. Man cloathed by us grows proud, when we
are neither proud nor adorned with our web ; though I
know not why this should be. Who more noble than
man ? and yet we are not unworthy to cover him.

FLAX.

Chosen to represent the Vegetables. Much labour to
prepare it. How flax is made into linen. The seed is
useful for medicine, and the oil from the seed for tempering
of colours, and in physic. The threads for binding and
tying, and for making linsey-wolseys, kersies, silks, &c.
But linen is the greatest product, used for shirts, for those
who wear woolen next skin are subject to filthy diseases.
In former times, when linen was not so plentiful, people
wasted much time in bathing, which occasioned so many
baths to be built in Rome and other places. Those who
did not use linen were liable to many diseases ; hence the

cleanliness of man due to linen. Therefore, owing to us, men spend less time in bathing, but have more time for graver occupations. Then linen is used for sails, hence for all navigations ; and books were and are sometimes made of linen. But when linen has become old, it is made into paper. What is calves-skins, sheepskins, or waxen-tablet compared to paper ? All learning due to books, which can be carried about. Arts and sciences advanced by them. The business of Kings transacted by means of paper. One friend enjoys another by paper.

No garment can be stitched together without thread. A book is made of paper ; the letters mostly of thickened linseed oil ; and the ink from paper burned black, or any other smoke made of linseed—hence a whole printed book from flax.

MERCURY.

By my means is that gold, scattered in the sediments of rivers or pools, collected together, and in like manner silver is gathered from the mines. Also employed for guilding and silvering ; also in fishing, for the light I throw out ; and in fourbishing of arms ; and for the better moving and poising of engines. Pulverized with gold or any other body (so it be not corrosive or noxious), I am the best purgative Nature hath given us. This dust has the name and attribute of *Aurelian*, and is a *Panchymagôgon* (a Generall Medicine). I shall give a particular discourse of all its uses. [Here follows a long account of its medicinal uses, and doses to be used in various diseases.] By certain processes, *i.e.*, by mixing mercury with certain salts, &c., I am turned into a poison called Præcipitate. Of itself, mercury is an antidote against the plague and other diseases. As a semi-metal, I am extremely useful to man. Tutia, useful in curing the eyes, &c. ; other semi-metals used for medicinal purposes, and for making artists' colours. The various uses of lead, in the metal-shop and in medicine, also for pipes, cisterns, &c. The uses of tin, for vessels, &c.,

and for medicine and in the colouring of potters. Copper, used for vessels, intruments, &c., and especially for bells and canons; the various uses of bells, and the wonders of machines of war. Iron, for all industries of war, and used by kings and princes against enemies; bolts, chains, scales, weights; joins together coaches, ships, houses; and produces nails, hammers, anvils, and things made by their means. Iron well purified is steel, which cuts the hardest things. Of iron is made saws, locks, to keep thieves out; fetters, bridges, &c., and all these by means of mercury. Iron also of great use in medicine. Silver, how esteemed by all; as money, gives motion to all things, life to the poor man. Silver is sought for all the world over, at great hazard; it gives power to all who have it. Gold, nothing so durable, strong in fire, of greater value or beauty; in gold is no corruption, no rottenness, or putrefaction; also used in medicine as a restorative to the heart. Gold therefore has the prerogative over all other precious things. Mercury hath blessed man with the art of printing, *i.e.*, by means of letters made of lead, tin, antimony; and, with the help of Flax as paper, and ink, make contemptible the goose's quill and the calf's hide. My sons—Iron, lead, and copper—are clogged with sulphurous matter; tin less so, silver less still, gold not at all. Let gold have the right of primogeniture, then silver, and so the rest; but let Mars or iron be the servant of all. By all of which, you will understand by what right I lay claim to that government which we debate.

THE JUDGE.

Having considered all things which you have severally said before me, though all your deserts are so great, yet I conceive one of you ought more especially to enjoy the Royal crown. You Calfe told us the great services you did to mankind; you Sheep no less; you also, Goose, must be lifted among these heroes; you, Oyster, are mistress of many rarities; none will despise thee, Bee, though small; who would not admire thee, Silkworm, for thy deserts; and

thee, Flax, for thy benevolences to the world ? But thou
Mercury so much exceeds thy competitors as the sun the
planets ; thou art the miracle, splendour, and light of the
world. Take thy recompence, the Royal Crown, declared
*The King of All Worldly Things Being under the
Command of Man;* which said, he was crowned with a
gold crown.

And thus the assembly, mad with anger and envy, yet
since the decree could not be reversed, returned each to his
home, everywhere proclaiming Mercury King ; and the
Judge retired home.

THE END.

EXAMEN FUCORUM PSEUDO-CHYMICORUM detectorum et in gratiam veritatis amantium succincte refutatorum, Authore Michaele Maiero, Com. Pal. Eq. Ex. Med. D.

Vignette represents an alchemic furnace in blast, and owl sitting nearby ; three men, elaborately dressed, holding on a rod various chemical implements towards the worker at the furnace ; behind the men a hive into which bees are flying, &c. Francofurti Typis Nicolai Hoffmanni, sumptibus Theodori de Brij, anno MCDXVII. Epigramma authoris on back of title. Dedication, 4 pp : work, 7-47 ; A²-F³. —AUTHOR'S LIBRARY.

The author, in his epigram, holds up to scorn the drones —false chemists—who impose upon those willing to learn the art, of which the professed teachers are themselves ignorant.

This little work is dedicated to Joachim Hirschberger, doctor of medicine, a most diligent chemical student, and the author's particular friend. Although his friend might be preoccupied in graver matters, yet the notoriety of the disease which the writer now attacks—the agility, the audacity of those drones, who, instead of gathering honey, destroy the labours of others—requires to be exposed. The dedication is dated at Francfurt in the month of September 1616. Follows 2 pp. of preface to the benignant reader. Describing the nature of the drones in the bee-hives—lazy and greedy—he compares the pseudo-chemist with these pretending but useless bees. They are but as the Sirens and Harpies who attempted to attract Ulysses.

The " Examen " opens with the story of Helicon, in

which the famous stone, thrown up by Saturn, as related
by Hesiod, is to be found :—

> " A stone the mother gave him to devour ;
> Greedy he seiz'd the imaginary child,
> And swallowed heedless, by the dress beguiled ;
>
> .   .   .   .   .   .
>
> By earth thy art, and Jove his powerful son,
> The crafty Saturn, one by gods ador'd,
> His inspired offsprings to the light restor'd,
> First from within he yielded to the day
> The stone deceitful, and his latest prey,
> Then Jove, in memory of the wondrous tale,
> Fixed on Parnassus in a sacred vale."

But the ascent to the sacred mount is both difficult and
arduous. Of those difficulties to be surmounted before the
top be reached "dictum est in Symbolis Aureæ Mensæ."
To those who are wandering about the sides of the sacred
mount will be given the string by which Ariadne will give
them, so that in the " Viatorium," the seven gates which
lead to " Montes Planetarum" will be opened to philosophers
and learned men. The rest, who are but in the lower
places, partly from laziness, " pigrique ventres," partly from
stupidity, run the wrong way and become the prey of
designing and ignorant guides.

The author, therefore, in this " Examen" desires to
point out and warn those simpler ones against those
pseudo leaders who desire only to make victims of the
unwary, calling themselves chemists. Prudence shows that
it is necessary to learn how to distinguish between good
and bad, the legitimate and illegitimate, the true and false.
But how is the distinction to be made ? Can those who
live a life of riot, whose life is impure, be fit guides or
instructors ? But that such pseudo-chemists have always
existed, and that those who are learning need to be warned
against them, we find from Geber and Albertus Magnus.
The true artificer in the work is of a good nature, ingenious ; and by assiduity, learning, work, through books,
by temperance, probity, and vigilance, will be able to
accomplish what is desired. On the other hand, the pseudo-
chemist will be known by luxury, impiety, falsehood, and

by laziness and the small amount of his learning. The author goes on to distinguish four sorts of chemical drones. There are those who may know a little of the theory of the art, yet have no practical knowledge. Those, too, who being poor, promise to perform what they have no means to perform. Then there are those who, by vulgar ostentations, display as of mighty importance some small secrets, which they desire or attempt to magnify by great ceremonies. Then there are the real impostors, who, by fraud, by theft and wicked impositions, having gained the means from their victims, seek refuge in flight or dishonesty.

Cunradius (that is Khunrath) is quoted by Maier in several cautions which he has laid down, which inform the unwary of the tricks of the "fuci." Cornelius Agrippa and "Scotus ille Italicus" are also quoted. Some extraordinary experiments are named, which are attributed to the "fuci" by Conrad, Crollius, and others. It has been said, and perhaps with some measure of truth, that Maier himself was at one time victimised by some of those "fuci," and that in their impostures he wasted both his means and his health.

JOCUS SEVERUS, hoc est Tribunale æquum quo Noctua Regina Avium, Phœnice arbitro post varias disceptationes et querelas Volucrum eam infestantium pronunciatur, et ob sapientiam singularem, Palladi sacrata agnoscitur : Authore Michaele Maiero Com. Pal. M.D.

[Vignette of the various birds.] Francofurti. Typis Nicholai Hoffmanni, sumptibus Theodori de Brij, anno, MDCXVII ; pp. 76 ; 4to. —BRITISH MUSEUM.

The assemblage of the birds includes the owl, the crow, the goose, the crane, the raven, the nightingale, the jackdaw, the heron, the swallow, the sparrow-hawk, the cuckoo, &c. They meet in equal degree, and after debates and disputes, the owl, the bird of Minerva, receives the place as queen. The singular wisdom of that famous bird carries off the crown. The Phœnix presides at the meeting.

The work is addressed (in a dedication " written on his road from England to Bohemia"), " Omnibus veræ chymiæ amantibus per Germaniam," and amongst them more especially, " illi ordini adhuc delitescenti, at Fama Fraternitatis et Confessio sua admiranda et probabili manifesto." This work, it appears, had been written in England.[1]

[1] De Quincy, " Inquiry," works iii., 397-398.

SILENTIUM POST CLAMORES, hoc est, Tractatus Apologeticus, quo causæ non solum clamorum seu Revelationem Fraternitatis Germanicæ de R. C. sed et Silentii; seu non redditæ ad singulorem vota responsionis, una cum malevolorum refutatione, traduntur et demonstrantur, scriptus Authore Michaele Maiero Imperialis consistorij comite, Eq. Ex. Phil. et Med. D. Francof. apud Lucam Iennis. MDCXVII.

8vo ; pp. 142 [2 blank] ; vignette. This was translated into German, Franckfurt, 1617 ; 8vo ; pp. 150 [2 blank]. The second edition of the Latin was published at Frankfurt, 1622 ; 8vo ; pp. 236 [4 blank]. At p. 101 begins a reprint of Themis Aurea, with a separate title-page, 1624. See Gardner Bib. Ros., 463 (German edition) ; also Ferguson's Bibl. Chem., 64.

—BRITISH MUSEUM.
— BODLIEAN LIBRARY [1624 ed.]

In this work the author professes to explain why the Rosicrucian Order treats its applicants with silence. " The author asserts that from very ancient times philosophical colleges have existed among various nations for the study of medicine and of natural secrets, and that the discoveries which they made were perpetuated from generation to generation by the initiation of new members, whence the existence of a similar association at that present time was no subject for astonishment. The philosophical colleges referred to are those of old Egypt, whose priests in reality were alchemists, ' seeing that Isis and Osiris are sulphur and *argentum vivum*'; of the Orphic and Eleusinian mysteries, of the Samothracian Cabiri, the Magi of Persia, the Brachmans of India, the Gymnosophists, Pythagoreans,

F

&c. He maintains that one and all of these were instituted, not for the teaching of exoteric doctrines, but the most arcane mysteries of Nature. Afterwards he argues that if the German Fraternity had existed, as it declares, for so many years, it was better that it should reveal itself, than be concealed for ever under the veil of silence, and that it could not manifest itself otherwise than in the ' Fama' and ' Confessio Fraternitatis,' which contain nothing contrary to reason, nature, experience, or the possibility of things. Moreover, the Order rightly observes that silence which Pythagoras imposed on his disciples, and which alone can preserve the mysteries of existence from the prostitution of the vulgar. The contents of the two manifestoes are declared to be true, and we are further informed that we owe a great debt to the Order for their experimental investigations, and for their discovery of the universal Catholicon. The popular objections preferred against it are disposed of in different chapters, *e.g.*, the charges of necromancy and superstition. The explicit statement of the Society, that all communications addressed to it should not fail to reach their destination, although they were unknown and anonymous, proving apparently false, was a special cause of grievance : those who sought health and those who coveted treasures at their hand were equally disappointed, and, according to Michael Maier, appear to have been equally enraged. He expostulates with them, saying, ' Non omnis ad omnia omnibus horis paratus est,' but his arguments as a whole can hardly be deemed satisfactory. ' Locorum absentia, personarum distantia,' &c., could scarcely prove obstacles to men who were bound by no considerations of space and time, and readers of the inmost heart would have discovered some who were worthy among the host of applicants." [1]

" Nature is yet but half unveiled. What we want is chiefly experiment and tentative inquiry. Great, therefore, are our obligations to the Rosicrucians for labouring to

[1] Waite, "History of the Rosicrucians," iii., pp. 269-271.

supply this want. Their weightiest mystery is a Universal Medicine. Such a Catholicon lies hid in Nature. It is, however, no simple but a very compound medicine. For out of the meanest pebbles and weeds, medicine, *and even gold,* is to be extracted. . . He that doubts the existence of the R. C. should recollect that the Greeks, Egyptians, Arabians, &c., had such secret societies ; where, then, is the absurdity in their existing at this day ? Their maxims of self-discipline are these—To honour and fear God above all things ; to do all the good in their power to their fellow-men"; and so on. " What is contained in the Fama and Confessio is true. It is a very childish objection that the brotherhood have promised so much and performed so little. With them, as elsewhere, many are called but few chosen. The masters of the order hold out the rose as a remote prize, but they impose the cross on those who are entering. . . Like the Pythagoreans and Egyptians, the Rosicrucians exact vows of silence and secrecy. Ignorant men have treated the whole as a fiction ; but this has arisen from the five years' probation to which they subject even well-qualified novices before they are admitted to the higher mysteries ; within this period they are to learn how to govern their tongues." [1]

[1] De Quincey, " Inquiry," iii., pp. 398, 399.

SYMBOLA AUREÆ Mensae duodecim nationum. Hoc est, Hermæa seu Mercurii Festa ab Heroibus duodenis selectis, artis Chymica usu, sapientia et authoritate Paribus celebrata, ad Pyrgopolynicen seu Adversarium illum tot annis iactaubundum, virgini Chemiæ Iniuriam argumentis tam vitiosis, quam convitiis argutis inferentem, confundendum et exarmandum, Artifices vero optime de ea meritos suo honori et famæ restituendum, Ubi et artis continuatio et veritas invicta 36, rationibus, et experientia librisque authorum plus quam trecentis demonstratur, Opus, ut Chemiæ, sit omnibus aliis Antiquitatis et rerum scitu dignissimarum percupidis, utilissimum, 12 libris explicatum et traditum, figuris cupro incisis passim adiectis, authore Michaele Maiero Comite Imperialis Consistorii, Nobili, Exempto, Med. Doct. P. C. olim Aulico Cæs. Francofurti Typis Antonii Hummii, impensis Lucæ Iennis. MDCXVII.

Title surrounded by 12 oval portraits, with portrait of the author. 4to ; pp. 621. Dedication, 5 pp. ; poems in honour of author, 5 pp. ; preface, 7 pp. ; index authorum, 6 pp. ; index rerum, 36 pp. ; 1 p. errata. (:) 2—(:) (:) (:) A—Ooo3. Woodcut, p. 345 ; and woodcuts expressive of the different workers.

—AUTHOR'S LIBRARY.

The "Symbola" is the largest work which Maier has left us. It is full of the results of research, and interesting, though perhaps rather exhausting from its bulk. It is dedicated to Ernest, Count of Holsatia, Schaumburg, Sternberk,

&c. It commences with the encomiums of Socrates and Heracletus, goes on to the praise of "Chemia," who has reigned in Europe, Africa, and Asia ; whose subjects are to be found in every nation ; those nations may differ in habits, language, manners, religion, laws, and other institutions. "Amicus Socrates, Amicus Plato, veritas magis amica." At the Golden Table only truth can preside. It was therefore most necessary that an arbiter should preside in the meeting, one of splendid descent, judicious, ingenious, and not averse to the encouragement of the Muses. To that position he calls the Count of Holsatia. He had, " sub manu languida," brought forth this work, and now dedicated it to his patron. The defence of Chemia would be now safe. The dedication is dated at Frankfurt, Dec. 1616.

The portrait follows; it is reproduced as a frontispiece to this work, and is accompanied by poems addressed to the author by four different persons. The first, by Petrus Finxius, Med. D., begins :—

> " Sic Maiere, suos tibi cum Natura recessus
> Pandat, et immersum gurgite quicquid habet."

Others are very laudatory, and the whole concludes with two epigrams by the author himself, of considerable length. The preface " ad lectorem " follows.

It had been an ancient custom among the Romans to celebrate triumphs at a Golden Table, with its furniture of that precious metal. Then we read of Lucius Verus, when he had returned from Syria to Rome, holding such a celebration with twelve guests. Magnificent presents followed the entertainment.

Nothing is so praiseworthy, so sublime, as Chemia—the very science of sciences, the art of arts. What needs, receives, greater attention by its friends. Not merely day by day, but nightly studies, labours, are continued from time to time. Precious treasures result from these labours. To the court of Chemia, to the Golden Table, philosophic workers are now invited. Those who entered the halls of Ilium were associated with the dead, but here the invitation is to associate with those distinguished by innocence and purity of life. The author gives four reasons for writing his book. 1. The antiquity and the widespread fame of Chemia in different nations and places deserved to be recorded and better known. 2. Its true authors, practisers, and writers should be rescued from malevolent and untrue aspersions. 3. That the adversaries of the art should be known, the fallacy of their sayings should be indicated, so that the true place of Chemia, as the Queen of the Arts, should be duly upheld, and the truth of her labours for thousands of years recorded. May the Father of lights shower down all good and perfect gifts on those who vindicate the chastity of this virginal science. The Golden Table is round, " ex duabus Hemicycliis compacta, quarum una ruberrimi coloris, altera nivei visa est."

1. *Hermes, King of Egypt.*—Motto, " Sol est ejus conjugii Pater, et alba Luna Mater, tertius succedit. ut gubernator, Ignis." The woodcut represents Hermes pointing to the sun and moon, separated, yet nearly surrounded, by a flame of fire.

Hermes was not a fictitious person, but is mentioned in ancient Arabian histories. He is to preside at the banquet as the viceroy of Queen Chemia. But Hermes was the most ancient of the Egyptian philosophers, called Trismegistus, or a threefold wisdom. Jamblicus, Suidas, Apuleius, Pythagoras, all speak of Hermes. He lived near the time of the patriarch Abraham, to whom, some say, he was related. He derived his wisdom through Seth, the son of Adam, purely and uncorrupted. Jamblicus tells us he wrote many works on subjects of science. To us there have come his " Pomander" and "Asclepius." The Smaragdine Table was translated into Latin five hundred years ago. By tradition from Hermes we have received the knowledge of the doctrine of the Holy Trinity. Of it he thus speaks—" Fuit Lumen Intelligens, ante Lumen intelligens, et fuit super mens mentis lucida." In "Asclepius" he makes mention of the " chemic gods."

Hermes was acknowledged by Socrates. He called God the Highest, and the creator of the celestial gods.

The chemic art was handed down in Egypt in two ways—by the hieroglyphics engraved, and by the stories concerning the gods.

Gold is really worshipped. What labours, changes, watchings, exile, and distresses will men undergo for this earthly good—to obtain gold.

" Pauperiem fugiens currit mercator ad Indos, Et, O cives, cives quærenda pecunia primum, Virtus post mummos."

After his death, Hermes was worshipped in Egypt. No doubt it was the knowledge of the chemic art that prolonged the lives of the antediluvian patriarchs. But natural causes asserted, principally the infusion of the seminal fluid in its highest vigour and efficacy. It was Alexander the Great who found the Smaragdine Tablet in the grave of Hermes; so, at least, Albertus Magnus writes. Many chemic secrets are contained in the table. Maier continues his dissertation on the Tablet. He goes on to speak of a statement by Paul the Deacon of the discovery in the reign of Diocletian of books found in Egypt, teaching the chemic art, and the explanation of the word " Chemia"—" est auri et argenti confectio." Maier then tells the story of the Phœnix as related by Tacitus—its appearance at Thebes, sacred to the sun, its mouth and feathers quite different from those of other birds. The Egyptians, by the Phœnix, really understood the golden tincture. The fellow-workers, " congentiles," of Hermes were—Mena, Busiris, Simandius, Sesostris, Miris, Chemnis, Sethon, Amasis, Adfar Alexandrinus, the tutor of Morien; King Calid, who learned the art from Morien.

The chemic art in the Egyptian colonies. The Phœnician, Cadmus, the founder of Thebes in Bœotia, where he slew the dragons Typhon and Echidna, and scattered the dragon-teeth—an arcane story referring to the art. The work of Tyre, multiplying silver and making idols of gold —which the Rabbis interpret as referring to arts of a

secret nature. Ths priests of Belus in Babylon were
devoted to astrology and philosophic work, and from
Egypt were the teachers of the Eleusinian mysteries
brought. On the borders of Egypt, too, was the Sphinx.
Its enigma referred to our subject.

Amongst the Ethiopians was the college of Gymnosophists; and in the year of Christ 40, Apollonius Tyanæus,
a philosopher of admirable life and doctrine, visited it.

Amongst the Persians was the college of the Magi.
Magic is not evil, though " negromantia," the intercourse
with evil spirits, was known in that country. The fame of
the Persian magi is referred to by Cicero and Strabo.
Natural magic is chemic, and teaches the arcane nature
of medicines.

Then there was the college of Brachmans in India. Of
it Apollonius also speaks. He travelled thither. In this
college of wise men, eighteen in number, Iarchas was
president. These believe in a metempsychosis. They also
held that the earth was really an animal, capable of
production. Belus had a human head, but as to the rest of
his body, resembled a lion. They knew also the secret of
the "aqua auri," and of the magnetic stone. They had an
image of Tantalus holding a phial of the incorruptible
water, of which Apollonius is said to have drunk. Tantalus is the representative of chemic art.

Chemia and Hermes then offer certain syllogistic
puzzles and questions. These are sustained, denied, and
affirmed. An example :—

" 3. Argumentum Chemiæ contradicentium
        Si ex metallo corrupto generaretur metallum daretur circu-
        laris generatio."
    " At hæc non datur.
    Ergo ex metallo corrupto non generatur metallum.
    Hermetis Responsio.
    Propositiones maioris connectio nulla est," &c.

The particulars known and disputed as to Hermes may
be conveniently studied in Jennings' edition of " The
Divine Pymander," by Dr Everard, Lon. 1884 ; introduction and essay. Works, &c., and references, Ferguson's

"Bibliotheca Chemica," *in voce* Hermes ; "Isis Unveiled," Blavatsky, *in voce.*

The second seat at the banquet is assigned to *Maria Hebræœ,* whose motto given is "Fumus complectitur fumum et herba alba crescens super monticulis capit utrumque." The woodcut shows Maria (said by some to be the same as Miriam, sister of Moses) pointing to a little hill on which grows a five-flowered plant ; below the hill is a vase, out of which smoke rises ; beyond the plant another vase is placed downwards, from which or into which smoke also issues or ascends ; the smoke breaks into two parts, united again at the top ; between these is the " herba alba" seen.

" During the sojourn at Memphis of Democritus, he is said to have become associated with a Hebrew woman named Maria, remarkable at that period for the advance she had made in philosophy, and particularly in the department of the Hermetic Art. A treatise, entitled 'Sapientissima Maria de Lapide Philosophica Præscripta,' is extant ; also ' Maria Practica,' a singularly excellent and esteemed fragment, which is preserved in the alchemical collections." [1]

" She gets the credit of having invented or introduced the use of the water-bath, which to this day is known as ' Balneum Mariæ,' or ' Bain-Marie.' "

Maier holds that Moses can be proved to be a " worker," as his wonderful ark, overlaid with gold, can testify. He gave the specimens and directions to the workers of the Tabernacle ; and did he not cause the crushed remains of the golden calf to be dissolved in water and drunk by the people ? Abraham and Joseph also knew the art. Solomon was a proficient. He had all wisdom from God. Chemia is wisdom, therefore he had that part necessarily. He had all riches, and a vast store of gold and silver. The King of Tyre was associated with him, to whom the Phœnicians were traders and mechanics. The Queen of Sheba also

---

[1] " Suggestive Inquiry," 12 ; see also Ferguson's Catalogue, *in voce.*

brought gold and gems. So the ancient secrets of practical
art were in his possession, and came by descent to the
possession of Maria, who wisely concealed their true meanings in her books. The arcane keys and ring of Solomon
are celebrated by innumerable ancient writers. Amongst
the " congentiles Hebræi" are Calid, Musa, Hamech, Isaac,
" Johannes quoque Evangelista. . . Qui de virgis fecit
aurum, gemmas de lapidibus." He describes the new
Jerusalem as paved with the purest gold. That purest
gold has in it the " Tinctura philosophia," of which then he
knew the secret. The usual syllogistic questions and
answers follow.

Democritus holds the next place at the Table. His
motto is " Pharmaco ignito spolianda densi est corporis
umbra." The woodcut represents him pointing to a
female, nearly naked, holding in her hand a burning heart,
while behind is a man, his one hand on a hammer, the
other holding a cup of fire, which he seems to be emptying
on the ground. Democritus represents Greece. He had
travelled in Egypt and India. He was greatly esteemed
by famous men who succeeded him. Celsus gives him the
name of the Great Philosopher. Mirandulanus thus speaks
of Democritus—" Supra centum vixit annos, multa depre-
hendit, quæ literatorum vulgus latuere : scribebat autem
sub obscure præcepta." He learned astrology and theology
from the Magi and Chaldeans, and having in Ethiopia held
intercourse with the Gymnosophists, learned many arcane
secrets from them. He excelled in the knowledge of the
anatomy of animals. Instead of, like Heracletus, weeping
for the vanity of men and the changeableness of fortune, he
laughed at these. It was Orpheus, also, no doubt, a philosophic worker, who " primus de Vellere aureo allegoriam
pulcherrimam descripsit."

Maier goes on to details already referred to, in connection with the Eleusinian Mysteries, the ancient Grecian
games, and the lives of Grecian heroes, writers, and philo-

sophers. The account of Apollonius is interesting. The writing of Psellus on rhetoric, history, mathematics, "sed et Physica, Medica et Chemica," are referred to. Synesius and Seneca are pressed into the list of "workers." The usual "Argumenta et Responsiones" are added.

The next alchemist is *Morien*, representing the Roman philosophic age. The woodcut represents him pointing to a man treading on a dung-heap, and behind a naked man falling backwards out of a window. The motto is—"Hoc accipe, quod in Sterquiliniis suis calcatur; si non, absque scala ascensurus cades in caput."

Morien is the first of Christian adepts. He was a solitary—a recluse. Hearing of Adfar, a philosopher of Alexandria, he went to that city, seeking his acquaintance and friendship. They studied together. After his death, he settled near Jerusalem, in company with a pupil. Kalid, the King of Egypt, having obtained possession of Adfar's MSS., found in them a treatise containing the secret of the Philosopher's Stone. Unable himself to understand the directions, Morien came to his rescue, and having perfected the work, inscribed these words on the vase in which he placed the treasure—"Omnis qui secum omnia habent, alieno auxilio nullatenus indigent." Morien afterwards returned to Kalid, and is said "to have discovered to him the secret of the transcendal science," but did not accomplish his conversion to the Christian religion, the thing he most desired. Maier continues this number with an account of the Roman studies, the story of the Phœnix given by Tacitus, the "copulatio" of Venus and Mars, "hoc est fæmina albæ et viri rubei conjunctio fieri debet in toto opere." Vesta "ignis est"—an Egyptian goddess. Even Cleopatra is pressed into service, for remember she knew how to dissolve the pearl in vinegar, and then drank it. Maier gives the Bononian epitaph, and explains that all its contradictory claims relate to the properties of the universal subject.[1]

[1] "Suggestive Inquiry," 19.

"ÆLIA LÆLIA CRISPIS.

" Nor male, nor female, nor hermaphrodite,
Nor virgin woman, young or old ;
Nor chaste, nor harlot, modest hight,
But all of them you're told.
Not killed by famine, poison, sword,
But each one had its share,
Not in heaven, earth, or water broad,
It lies, but everywhere."

"LUCIUS AGATHO PRISCUS.

" No husband, lover, kinsman, friend,
Rejoicing, sorrowing, at life's end,
Knows or knows not, for whom is placed
This — what ? This pyramid so raised and graced,
This grave, this sepulchre ? 'Tis neither,
'Tis neither— but 'tis all and each together.
Without a body, I aver,
This is in truth a sepulchre ;
But notwithstanding, I proclaim
Both corpse and sepulchre the same."

Another epitaph is quoted, and a reference made to the
ever-burning lamps of antiquity. Psyche, Cupid, the
golden ass, for Apuleius translated Hermes into Latin ; the
golden bough in the Æneid—" Nunc adversarii argumenta
expectantur," &c.

"*Avicenna*, Arabicæ gentis Princeps, quinto loco con-
sederat." The woodcut is that of the Arabian sage
pointing to the flying eagle held down to earth by the
creeping toad. The motto—"Aquila volans per aerem et
Bufo gradiens per terram est Magisterium."

Avicenna was an Arabian or a Mauritanian. Not
merely was he learned in the sciences as taught under
Mahometan rule, but also famous for his knowledge in
occult and hidden arts. The Saracens had all books of
science from Greece and Egypt translated into Arabic.
Like Hippocrates and Galen, Avicenna was deeply learned
in medical science He wrote on these subjects, and
obtained the name of Avicenna Princeps. He commenced
the study of medicine at the age of sixteen. Yet it is said
that he was " a philosopher devoid of wisdom," for he lost
his position of Grand Vizier through his disorderly life,

and died at the age of fifty-six. Six or seven Hermetic
treatises are ascribed to him. Maier speaks at some length
of the position and beliefs of the followers of Mahomet
compared with the beliefs of Christians. That Mahomet
himself was instructed in letters is certain ; and who has
not heard of " the gold of Arabia "? In the woods of
Arabia the Phœnix dwells till he come to Egypt. At
Damascus was a celebrated college of all kinds of learning.
Avicenna's " Tractatulus de Alchemia," and his treatise on
the " Congelation of the Stone," are well known. He tells
us that " Res, cujus caput est rubeum, oculi nigri, et pedes
albi, est magisterium." In his motto the Eagle, which flies
in the air, denotes the moon ; the Toad denotes a very
opposite element. It loves the earth ; this refers to the
firm and philosophic, the base and foundation upon which
the golden house is built. From the toad, treated with
vinegar, macerated and dried, is made a philosophic medicine, good against the plague, poison, and other diseases.

The " congentiles " of Avicenna are Geber, Artephius,
Alphidius, Gilgil, Hamuel, Rhasis, and a very large number
of others, all named.

The usual conclusion of syllogistic questioning and
response follows.

The sixth alchemist represents Germany, and is *Albertus
Magnus*. His motto is—" Omnes concordant in uno, qui
est bifidus." The woodcut represents the abbot, duly
vested, pointing to a Hermaphrodite, or a bi-sexual per-
sonage, with a male and female head, and bi-sexual organs.
He holds a Y in his right hand.

Albert was a universal genius. His works are contained
in twenty-one folio volumes. His character has been given
as " great in magic, greater in philosophy, greatest in
theology." There is no doubt but that he was a hermetic
student. His experiments are recorded in the " Secretum
Secretorum," first printed in 1508. Maier tells that in
chemia Albert was a hard worker and student, a great and

perfect "chemicus." He says also that he received from St Dominic the secret of the Philosophical Stone, that he communicated it to St Thomas Aquinas, that he constructed an automaton which was endowed with the power of speech, and served as an oracle—the android which St Thomas destroyed, believing it to be a work of the devil. He had travelled through many regions, visited many provinces and cities. There is no reason to doubt his acquaintance with much that was then little known in regard to the properties of minerals and metals. He was properly called "the Great." The stories about him are endless, but there is no reason to believe that he was the author of the "Grimoire" which has been attributed to him. His "congentiles" are Trevisan, Basil Valentinian, well known as the author of the "Triumphal Chariot of Antimony"; Isaac Holland, Pontanus, also the author of the "Rosary," and the great Paracelsus, of whom Maier gives a long and interesting account.

After this comes an account of "Collegium Philosophorum Germanorum R.C." A number of "dubia," eight in number, are given as to the Rosicrusians, with answers by Maier to these doubts. Follows "Ænigmata a IX. Musis et Apolline de Collegio Germanorum Philosophorum R.C." The article ends in the usual form. Albert died at Cologne, 1280." [1]

The French alchemist next appears. He is *Arnold Villanovanus*—born probably about 1245, according to one account; but flourished in the time of the Emperor Ludovick Bavarus (1314-1346), according to Maier. His motto is—"Lapis habetur ex Matrimonio Chabrici et Beiæ." The woodcut represents the marriage. Arnold excelled in medicine, chemia, and astrologia. He was particularly expert in chemia. His books are—"Rosarius," "Lumen Luminum," "Epistola ad regem Neapolitanum," "Flos

[1] See Ferguson's Catalogue, "Bibliotheca Chemica," *in voce* "Albertus Magnus," for references.

Florum," and some more. Mirandula and others give Arnold a very high place. For ten years he journeyed through Italy, visiting different universities. But he was greatly persecuted. He died on the way going to Rome to excuse himself to the Pope. In his life he was good, pious, honest, constant, laborious, and in every way useful. In doctrine, a great theologian; in medicine, complete; in chemia and astrology, perfect. He had enemies, indeed, who may be compared to hyenas—eager to devour and to calumniate. They alleged that, for his evil life, he was lost in a storm, and his body never received Christian burial; but this axiom is a divine truth—" Qui bene vixit male mori non potest." An epitaph and an epigram are given. His congentiles include Flamel, Zacharius, Fernelius, and others. A curious "Ænigma de affinitate Metallorum," is given by Maier (p. 345) in shape of a Tree, with numbered or lettered branches. An article follows –" Gallorum honori"—in which a description of the country is given—its census, ecclesiastical state, its productions, the power of the " Pontifex Romanus"—therein.

Then follow the usual syllogistic questions. The first may be given :—

" CONTRA CHEMIAM.

" Si Natura non potest ex plumbo aurum facere, nec ars unquam faciet.
" At Natura id nequit
Ergo nec ars potest."

The Italian alchemists are represented by *Thomas Aquinas*, the eighth of the Golden Table. His motto is— " Ex Sulphure et Argento vivo, ut Natura, sic ars producit metalla." In the woodcut, he stands pointing to an artificial hill, cavernous in sight, from which the flames of Mars and Venus ascend. On the top is a worker tending a built furnace in operation.

Thomas Aquinas is said to have been the favourite pupil of Arnold. He is called " Doctor Angelicus." His writings are full of subtle questions in regard to divine and human affairs. That the books called by his name are genuine, Mirandulanus bears witness, and other chemists frequently cite his works. The "Rosary" quotes his saying that the most precious stones are those proceeding from animals. He describes "the Stone" as red, most clear, diaphanous, and lucid—"ex rubedine enim respexi formam ignis, ex diaphanitate formam aeris, et ex luciditate formam aquæ." In his descriptions of the "work," Thomas is particularly prudent. The power of natural magic is also admitted by him. "Metalla transmutari possunt unum in aliud, cum naturalia sint et ipsorum materia eadem." He refers to the powers and properties of antimony. "In the true Hermetic operation there is but one vase, one substance, one way, one only operation." His "congentiles" include Petrus Bonus, Petrus de Zalento, Marcellus Palingenius, and a large number more. "Italia laus" follows, and then the usual conclusions of reasonings, objections, and responses.

The ninth guest is *Raymund Lullius*, representing Spain. His motto is—"Corpus infantis ex masculo et Fœmina procedit in actum." The woodcut represents the parents teaching the child to walk. Lullius was one of the greatest of men, and exercised an influence on his generation now hardly realised. It is said that through his ascetic application and labours he received a special revelation from God of the universal science. Falling in love with a woman apparently very beautiful, but married, he followed her, till she took the unusual method of showing him her breast almost eaten away by a cancer. Shocked, saddened, but restored to his senses by this sight, he, in response to a vision of the Redeemer, afterwards assumed the habit of religion. He studied Arabic, with the intention of attempting the conversion of the followers of Mahomet. He became acquainted in Paris with Johannes Scotus. But some have supposed this Lullius to have been a different person from the alchemical writer.[1] Maier seems to hold that only one person of that name existed, who was the alchemist and author, as well as the theologian and ascetic. He appends an " Epigramma in Memoriam Raymundi Lullii" to his account, which is a pretty full one, of his labours and works :—

" Ad mensam parium doctos adjungis et illis
Offers Ambrosiam nectareosque cibos."

Cremer's " Testament," containing an account of Lullius' experiments in England, was first published by Maier about the year 1614, in his " Tripus Aureus." A " Ratio affirmativa ipsius Raymundi Lullii," appended to the " Symbola," is :—" Utrum alchemia sit ens reale, aut sit figmentum ?"[2]

The tenth guest is *Roger Bacon*—"Anglus." He stands in the woodcut with a pair of scales, equally poised, out of one of which flames are issuing. He is in a monkish habit, and has for his motto—" Elementorum fac aequationem et habebis." He is said to have been the first Englishman who cultivated the " work" of alchemy. He studied at Oxford and Paris. Settling at Oxford in 1257, he returned to Paris, where he was closely confined for ten years. At the request of Pope Clement IV., he wrote his " Opus Majus." Many of his alchemical MSS. still exist. It is said he died at Oxford about 1294. He acquired a reputation for magic, chiefly on account of his mechanical inventions. He has come down to us less as a philosopher than as a " brave necromancer, that can make women of devils, and juggle cats into costermongers."[3] Bacon was an astronomer also, and rectified the Julian Calendar. He is said to have invented spectacles. If he did not discover gunpowder, he contributed to its perfection.[4] Maier tells us " apparet itaque Baconem contradixisse Magiæ dia-

---

[1] See the account of this controversy in the " Lives of the Alchemystical Writers," by Waite, p. 82, *et seq.*
[2] See the very full references by Ferguson, *in voce*, " Bibl. Chemica."
[3] Ferguson's Cat., " Bib. Chem.," i. 65.
[4] Waite, "Alchem. Writers," 65, 66.

G

bolicæ." He was a great student of Avicenna. A list of
his " congentiles" follows—Garland, Ripley, who is said in
solitude to have written twenty-four books of different
kinds ; his " Twelve Gates of Alchemy" seems to prove
him an adept of the spiritual chemistry ; he therein declares
that the "principle" may be found everywhere ; Norton,
" chymicus perfectus," and the author of the " Ordinall of
Alchemy"; Cremer, Kelly, and the famous " Michael Scotus
in hoc quoque artificio in sua patria celebrari dicitur."
Very interesting is Maier's introduction here (p. 477) of
Norton's " De artificibus aliis Londini uno tempore congre-
gatis per decem dierum spacium." Maier adds—" Xenium
Angliæ gratitudinis ergo relictum." Giving an account of
the state of religion in England, Maier does not omit the
fact that St George is the national patron, and has some
remarks on the " Dragon," with which that saint is commonly associated. He very naturally thought it odd that
the crucifix and the pictures of the life of Christ having
been abolished from the churches, representations of the
" Dragon," " the Lion and Unicorn," should be found there ;
why images and organs should be found in the Royal
chapels and not in ordinary churches, when in Germany
pictures of Christ, the Blessed Virgin, and of saints are to
be seen in Lutheran churches. This part of the discussion
is interesting from the fact that it was the result, in all
probability, of the author's own observation. The usual
syllogistic encounters conclude the section.

The eleventh guest is *Melchior Cibinensis*, the Hungarian. His motto—" Lapis, ut Infans, lacte nutriendus
est Virginali." The woodcut represents Melchior saying
mass at an altar in full eucharistic vestments ; behind him,
in a flame, appears the Virgin sitting above a crescent
moon, giving the Holy Child milk from her right breast.
Melchior then was a priest, a man religious, and an arcane
student, an artificer in the " work." He saw the perfection
of it in the birth of the Philosophic Stone in the Sacred

Nativity; its sublimation in the life and passion; dark and black in the death; then in the resurrection and life, the red and perfect colour. This comparison he found in the nativity, life, passion, death, and resurrection of Christ as commemorated in the Eucharist. Thus earthly things are the pictures of the heavenly, " Lapis itaque ut Homo," born of two seeds, conceived, converted into the embryo, born into light, nourished by milk, growing to perfection, married, bearing the cross, dying, buried, laid in the grave, thence to rise and inherit life incorruptible.

Morien thus declares " Lapis noster est confectio ipsius magisterii et assimilatur in ordine creationi hominis . . . aperi ergo oculos tuos et vide." Four poems follow, and a list " adjuncti Melchiori," and the usual conclusions.

The twelth, the *"Anonymous"* guest. His motto is— " Saturnus humectat terram portantem Solis flores et Lunæ." The woodcut represents a man with a wooden leg, watering a number of trees, which amid their leaves bear suns and moons as flowers or fruit. Follows a list of anonymous authors and their works.

Then comes (p. 561) The Dessert—the Sweetmeat Course —the recapitulation and conclusions of the whole work. The world is still running after pomp and vanity, honours and luxury, placing its desire in riches, while Democritus laughs and Heraclitus weeps, and true are the words of Ecclesiastes—" Omnia vanitas vanitatum." My thoughts return from vanity to the sacred truths of the Holy Book, and amid all the confusion one arises, our Phœnix-bird, from whose ashes arises " Medicina omnium Medicinarum præsantissima." For there is the " Remedium Irae et Doloris, seu Nepenthes." The excellencies of this divine medicine are held forth at length, a long extract being given from Arnoldus, ex " libro de simplicibus." A mystical journey is now proposed, " sic enim Europa terræ, America aquæ, Asia aeris, et Africa Ignis imaginem et vires

optime repræsentat." The section referring to Asia is
specially interesting ; at page 589 a prayer is inserted—
" O summe et misericors Salvator mundi, Jesu Christe, qui
Deus ab eterno, homo factus es in tempore. . . Benedic
Medicinæ præclarissimo tuo dono." Under Africa, the
sayings of the Cumean Sybil are given from Eusebius, and
then Arabia Felix, the home of the Phœnix, is visited ; and
afterwards at Heliopolis " Ira et doloris remidium habeba-
tur." Poems follow in epigrammic form, " in honour of the
Erythræan Sybil, Mercury, to the Phœnix, and in honour
of the Hermetic Art." The work ends with " Hermetis
oratio gratiarum actoria." " May the Virgin Queen
Chemia be propitious and kind to us all." The whole
closes with the hymn, " Hermetis Regenerationis," from the
Pomander :—

> " Universa mundi natura hunc audiat hymnum.
> Audi terra, audite turbines imbrium O sylvæ silete, cantaturus
>   sum creatorem omnium, totum et unum.
> Audite cæli, quiescite venti, circulus Immortalis Dei orationem
>   istam exaudiat."

The writer feels the utter inadequacy of his description
of the " Symbola." In over 600 quarto pages Maier gives
an almost endless course of instruction in ancient learning.
The work may be justly considered as a supplement to the
"Arcana." At every point it is full of interest to the
student, scholar, antiquary, and reader of curious subjects.
The marvellous store of historical lore, the uncommon
pleasantries of style, the vastly different parts and subjects,
show the author to have been one of the greatest scholars
of his age. It is true that the subject is not a popular one,
but to the quiet student, lover of antiquity and history, the
volume is delightful in its fulness and its complexity. It
is a regular feast at the Golden Table, and its " Bellaria "
are welcome as the dessert.

ATALANTA FUGIENS, hoc est, Emblemata Nova de Secretis Naturæ Chymica, Accommodata partim oculis et intellectui, figuris cupro incisis, adjectisque sententiis, Epigrammatis et notis, partim auribus et recreationi animi plus minus 50 Fugis Musicalibus trium Vocum, quarum duæ ad unam simplicem melodiam distichis canendis peraptam, correspondeant, non absq; singulari jucunditate vivenda, legenda, meditanda, intelligenda, dijudicanda, canenda et audienda. Authore Michaele Majero Imperial. Consistorii Comite, Med. D. Eq. ex., &c. Oppenheimii, Ex typographia Hieronymi Galleri, Sumptibus, Joh. Theodori de Bry, MDCXVIII.

4to ; pp., 211 ; index fugarum, 1 p. ; monitio ad Philomusicum, 2 pp. ; portrait—50 engraved emblematic pictures, each with an epigram, which is set to music.
The first edition at Oppenheim, 1617 ; a different title-page, and where on page 11 (1618) a woodcut appears, this is blank in edition of 1617.   —Mr F. LEIGH GARDNER (Hopetoun bookplate.)

Short Title.—MICHAELIS MAJERI, Secreta Naturæ Chymica, nova plane subtilique methodo indagata.

Title.—MICHAELIS MAJERI, Imperial. Consistor. Comit. Med. D. Eq. Ex., &c. Secretioris Naturæ Secretorum Scrutinium Chymicum, per oculis et intellectui accurate accomodata, figuris cupro appositissime incisa, ingeniosissima Emblemata, hisque confines, et ad rem egregie facientes sententias, doctissimaque item Epigrammata, illustratum. Opusculum ingeniis altioribus, & ad majora natis, ob momenta in eo subtilia, augusta, sancta, rara, & alioqui nimium quantum abstrusa, quam maxime expetitum, desideratum ; Iterata vice amplissimæ Reipublicæ Chymicæ Bono & Emolumento, non sine singulari jucunditate, legendum, meditandum intelligendum, dijudicandum, depromptum. Francofurti, Impensis Georgii Henrici Oehrlingii, Bibliopolæ. Typo Johannis Philippi Andreæ. MDCLXXXVII.

4to ; pp. 150 ; preface to reader, 4 pp. more ; then rest A-T3. 50 symbolic engravings. The differences in this edition are the alteration of the title, the omission of the engraved title and Maier's portrait, the omission of the music, and of the " Epigramma Authoris" and " Epistola dedicatoria."

—HAIGH HALL LIBRARY.

Edition in German.—MICHAELIS MAJERI, Imperial. Consistor. Comit. Med. D. Eq. Ex., &c. Chymisches cabinet derer grossen Geheimnussen der Natur, durch wohl ersonnene sinnreiche Kupfferstiche und Emblemata, auch zu mehrerer Erleuchterung und Verstand derselben, mit angehefften sehr dienlich—und geschickten Sententien und Poëtischen Uberschrifften, dargestellet und ausgezieret. Welches, nachdeme es wegen vieler darinn entdeckten raren Geheimnussen und Erläuterung der Philosophischen Subtilitäten, von verschiedentlichen hocherleuchtenden und zu grossen Künsten sich applicirenden Liebhabern zum öffteren begehret und verlanget worden ; Der Chymischen Republic und dero Liebhabern, zur Speculation, Betracht —und Untersuchung aus wohlmeinender Veneration und Liebe zum zweyten mahl in der Lateinischen sprach

ausgefertiget, vor jetzo aber zum ersten mahl in das
Hochteutsche übersetzet ist, von G. A. K. der Philoso-
phischen Künsten Liebhabern. Deme beygefüget ist,
eine Application des Hohen Lied Salomonis, auff die
Universal-Tinctur der Philosophorum. Franckfurt,
Verlegts Georg Heinrich Oehrling, Anno 1708.

4to ; pp. [4] 153 [1 blank] ; 50 emblematic engravings.
—FERGUSON'S " BIBL. CHEMICA."

At the foot of the title-page of " Atalanta fugiens " is
shown the race of Atalanta and Hippomenes. The former,
swift and beautiful, was warned against marriage by an
oracle, and lived a lonely life in a forest. " She meets the
addresses of her suitors by challenging them to race with
her, and spearing them in the back. She is at length
beaten by Hippomenes, who, during the race, drops on the
ground three golden apples given him by Aphrodite.
Atalanta stoops down to pick up the apples, and thus
loses the race :—

> " The nimble Virgin, dazled to behold
> The glittering apple tumbling o'er the mold,
> Stop'd her career to seize the rowling gold."

" Hippomenes forgets to render thanks to Aphrodite [or
profanes the temple], and the goddess in anger causes the
pair to wander into a sanctuary of Cybele, where they are
changed into lions." [1]

At the side of the title-page, Venus is shown handing
the golden apples to Hippomenes ; at the bottom, Atalanta
is picking up one ; while Hippomenes is running with an
apple in each hand. Behind is a temple, the lovers in the
entrance embracing each other, while from behind they
issue as a lion and lioness. The upper part of the plate
represents Hercules with a club over his shoulder, clad in
a lion's hide, with the tail hanging so as to appear in the
natural position. He has arrived at the trees whereon

[1] Seyffert, *voce* "Atalanta."

hang the golden apples of Hesperides. He stretches out his hand to seize one. Up above appear Ægle, Arethusa, and Hespertusa. The title is pretty and well drawn. It has been very aptly remarked by one writer, that in the illustrated title-pages of Maier's works more information is communicated to the capable student than in whole volumes of other writers. On the back of the title is " Epigrammata Authoris," followed by a dedication to Christopher Reinart, doctor of laws, and Imperial Senator of Mülhausen, in Thuringia. As the tripod given by Vulcan to Pelops on his marriage was afterwards offered by him to the Pythian Apollo, and preserved at Delphi, becoming the seat wherefrom the Divine Oracles were declared, so the author, following the example of Pelops, consecrates his tripod to the use of that distinguished place from which he writes, and, before all other persons, to you, most excellent and noble, that he may give some public testimony of the benevolence which he had received a few years ago, in the time of the Emperor Rudolph, from the Medical Council of Frankfort. He hopes that his "Atalanta" may give his patrons, when they rest a little from their graver pursuits, recreation for both mind and hand, so that the author may still be kept in recollection, and numbered amongst the friends still dear to him and them. The dedication is dated, " Francofurti, ad Mænam, anno 1617, mense Augusto."

The preface contains a dissertation upon ancient music, and the story of Atalanta and Hippomenes, which is awanting in the " Secretioris Naturæ," but otherwise that second work is in the beginning and the end the same.

Maier tells us in the preface that Atalanta " virgo mere chymica est, et Hippomenes tanquam malo aurea in tertia tamen stabalimetur et firmantur, . . ex Hippomenes et Atalanta coeuntibus in templo Martis Deum, hoc est vase, fiunt liones, sive rubeum acquirent colorem." The story of Atalanta in her victory over the suitors, and in the killing of the wild boar, and receiving from Meleagar the head and hide of the monster as a prize, "apud stethæum Æsculapii fanum ē saxo percusso aquam elicuit quam sitibunda bibit"--all is explained in the Emblems. Each Emblem has three illustrations. First page—part of the epigram in verse set to music, in three voices— Atalanta, or the " vox fugiens"; Hippomenes, or the " vox sequens"; Pomum objectum, or the " vox morans." The epigram, in German, is at the bottom of the page. Second page—the emblem in figure, with the Latin verse at the foot ; then, in two pages, the discursus.

The emblems in all number fifty, and the plates in both editions are the same. According to Mr Waite ("Rosicrucians," 269), these quaint and mystical engravings "emblematically reveal the most unsearchable secrets of Nature."

Probably the most curious picture is Emblem No. 34, in which the Sun and Moon, represented in human form, are represented in the act of coition, standing in a pool of water.

A few specimens from the work will now follow :—

1. The wind has taken him in the belly. Epigram — " The wind carried it in its belly, the nurse thereof is the earth." The fruit which lives, concealed in the wind—look that it is not unsuitably born before its time, but comes living to earth in right measure.

7. The bird flies young from the nest ; the bird falls back into the nest—" It ascends from earth to heaven, and again descends to earth." In a hollow rock the eagle has made his nest. Therein concealed, he nourishes his young. One feathered easily raises itself ; but the featherless cannot—so falls back into its nest.

8. Take the Egg and strike it with a glowing sword. This bird has an egg, which is to be carefully sought. The white surrounds the yellow yolk ; such burn prudently with a glowing sword. Seek help from Mars, the fire god.

Then will a young bird bore through. Fire and iron can destroy. Here see " the strength of superiors and inferiors."

11. Make Latona white, and tear up the books. No one knows properly the twin race born of Jove. It is the Sun and Moon. Yet black spots leave many traces—make Latona white in the face—free from all colour ; and that you may escape injury, tear up the books—" penetrates every solid thing."

13. The brass of the wise is water-seeking, and desires to be bathed seven times in the river, like the leprous Naaman in Jordan.

14. The Dragon eating its own tail. Hunger compels the many-footed fish to devour its foot. Many nourish themselves with the flesh of others, and so it does not vex the dragon to bite, even devour his tail, so that he even enjoys a part of his own body for food. He will be tamed by the sword, by hunger, and imprisonment, till he completely devours and recreates himself again. " The strongest of all fortitudes."

21. Make of man and woman a circle ; then a quadrangle ; out of this a triangle ; make again a circle, and you will have the Stone of the Wise. Thus is made the stone, which thou canst not discover, unless you, through diligence, learn to understand this geometrical teaching.

23. Gold rains while Pallas is born at Rhodes, and the sun lies by Venus. It is a wonderful thing, so the Greeks teach us as true, which at Rhodes took place in the ancient time. They say that a fruitful rain of gold fell. As the sun has lain by Venus in love, also as out of the forehead of Jove did Pallas come, so also in thy vessel must gold show its elf-like rain.

25. The Dragon does not die, but is really killed by his

brother and sister, which are the sun and moon. The Dragon may, unless the art be more than slight, begin to live and again creep out. His brother and sister strike his head with clubs. This is the only way he can be killed. Apollo is the brother, and Diana the sister.

29. As the Salamander lives in the fire, so does the Stone. The Salamander lives, strong and unhurt, in the strong fire — so the cruel heat of the flames is but of small matter, for the Philosopher's Stone is born in the perpetual fire. It is uninjured, becoming cold out of the fire. It stands in equal heat with the Salamander.

35. As Ceres, Triptolemus, and Thetis Achilles became accustomed to linger under the fire, so will the maker of the Stone. The fire is as the milk from the breast of the mother—nourishment for the medicine of the wise.

41. Adonis is killed by a wild boar. Venus, hastening to help, colours the roses with Adonis' blood. Myrrha has given birth to Adonis, by her own father, whom Venus greatly loves. He is killed by a wild boar, and Venus, running to his assistance, hurts her leg by a rose branch, so by her blood the white rose becomes red. She weeps with the Syrians, and soon lays him to rest under the soft lettuce—

"Illum lactuis mollibus et posuit."

43. Atalanta listens to the Vulture, which does not speak falsely. On the high summit of the mountain, the Vulture sits screaming aloud without ceasing. I alone am the white and black, the lemon yellow and the red. I lie not. The raven also, flying, though his wings are cut off, in the dark night. It is out of this or that the whole art goes.

" These fifty plates, and the epigrammatic description of them, supply to the adept who holds the *Clavicula* a complete view of the system of the Universe, the essential unity of all things, the possible transmutation of matter, and the highest form of Theosophy able to be conceived by earthly mortals. (Quod Scis Nescis, 1866)." [1]

The "Atalanta" may be called a book of alchemistic or mystic proverbs. Everything in Nature is explanatory of or connected with "the Stone." For instance, the 39th emblem refers to the Coral. A man is fishing out a branch from the water. The epigram tells that the Coral, which grows under water, becomes hard when brought to air, "sic lapis."

Emblem 45 represents the earth in space, with the motto—"Sol et ejus umbra perficiunt opus."

The whole earth, then, lies between the Sun and Moon, and the influence of Sol and his shadow are everywhere felt. Silver is but the shadow of gold, and the Dragon must become as the Salamander in the fire, impervious to heat, yet at the same time fully operated on by the influence of its power.

Man, then, has in his body the anatomy of the whole world, and all his members answer to some celestial influences. So the adepts describe the life of man, as by their art revealed, to be a pure, naked, and unmingled fire of infinite capability.

"Man, then, shall we conclude at length, is the true laboratory of the Hermetic art, his life the subject, the grand distillatory, the thing distilling, and the thing distilled, and self-knowledge is at the root of all alchemical tradition." [2]

Philo declares that the soul of man is but an impression of the Seal of the Logos. All the emblems, then, of Maier's "Atalanta" have a meaning beyond that of crucible, fire, and ore. They are mystic, spiritual, and the reflex of a higher and nobler nature. He desires to teach us, not merely of gold and silver under Sol and Luna, of the black matter under the story of the dragon, of the red tincture as colouring the roses at the death of Adonis, but of greater

[1] Gardner, "Bibl. Rosa.," 49.   [2] "Sug. Inquiry," 153.

and deeper things. He teaches us, in the words of the authors of the " Suggestive Inquiry," that the Father can only be discovered in perfect quiet approach to the cause of all. That in drawing near to the Deity, although no eye can penetrate that fire which is his circumference, that yet when the light in the purified soul meets the eternal light of God, then the whole intelligible universe unfolds itself. The shell dissolves, and the magnificence of the pearl within is discovered. In the words of Böhme, " by death and contrition of the agent in the patient, and *vice versa*, the old life is finally crucified, and out of that crucifixion, by reunion of the principles under another law, the new life is elected, which life is a very real and pure quintessence—the mercury so much sought after, even the Elixir of Life, which needs only the corroborative virtue of the Divine Light, which it draws in order to become the living gold of the philosophers, transmuting and multiplicative, the concrete form of that which in the dead metal we esteem."

TRIPUS AUREUS, Hoc est, Tres Tractatus, Chymici Selectissimi, Nempe I. Basilii Valentini, Benedictini Ordinis monachi Germani, Practica una cum 12 clavibus et appendice, ex Germanico ; II. Thomæ Nortoni, Angli philosophi Crede Mihi seu Ordinale, ante annos 140, ab authore scriptum, nunc ex Anglicano manuscripto in Latinum translatum, phrasi cuiusque authoris ut et sententia retenta ; III. Cremeri cuiusdam Abbatis Westmonasteriensis Angli Testamentum, hactenus nondum publicatum, nunc in diversarum nationum gratiam editi, et figuris cupro affrabre incisis ornati opera et studio Michaelis Maieri Phil. et Med. D. Com. P., &c.

[A double illustration of, on the one side, a library, with the three authors in conversation, the abbot in the middle, holding a pastoral staff ; on the other half, a laboratory, in which is a furnace, which divides the pictures, and a smith, naked, except round the middle of his body, working at the fire.] Francofurti Ex Chalcographia Pauli Iacobi, impensis Lucæ Iennis, anno MDCXVIII ; 4to ; continuous pagination, 196 ; A²-B⁶,3. Dedication, "Dn. Ioanni Hartmanno Beyero, D.M.," 3 pp. ; portrait. First sub-title, p. 7, Practica cum Duodecim Claribus et Appendice, De Magno Lapide Antiquorum Sapientum, scripta et relicta a Basilio Valentino Germ. Benedictini ordinis monacho. Tractatus Primus [Cut of a monk holding and pointing to a pair of scales, equally balanced, one flaming, the other still.] Francofurti apud Iennis. Second sub-title, page 77, Thomæ Nortoni Angli Tractatus Chymicus Dictus Crede Mihi Seu Ordinale. Tractatus Secundus. [Cut of a man with sword at side, pointing to a child which father and mother are holding by the arms, teaching it to walk.] Francofurti apud Iennis. Opposite is a sort of frontispiece printed on the back of the last page of preceding treatise ; upper part represents a chemical furnace, underneath, in three compartments, eight beasts and birds ; first three—Lion, Eagle, and Serpent—are crowned. Third sub-title of the blank leaf, p. 183—

Testamentum Cremeri, Abbatis Westmonasteriensis, Angli, Ordinis Benedictini. Tomus Tertius. [Cut representing the abbot pointing to a huge tent, like open-faced furnace, in which two flames are rising, and at the top outside is standing a man, watching the flame or smoke coming out of a furnace.] Francofurti apud Iennis. Reprinted in Musæum Hermeticum Reformatum, 1677 ; and again in 1749. The Hermetic Museum was translated into English by Arthur Edward Waite ; published, London, J. Elliot & Co., 1893 ; 2 vols. ; 4to. [250 copies.] Each treatise, " Balcarras " on vellum cover, front and back, in an oval arms in gilt, labelled " David Dominus Lyndesay De Balcarras." —HAIGH HALL LIBRARY.

CHYMISCHER TRACTAT THOMÆ NORTONI eines Engelländers Crede Mihi seu Ordinale genandt. vor ungesehr und erthalbhundert Jahren in Engelländischer Sprach Reimenweiss beschrieben, Nachmaln auss dem MSS. so zuvor niemals in Truck Rommen Von M. Maiero Lateinisch vertit, &c. ; 8vo. Frankfurt am Mahn, Lucæ Jennis, 1625. Collation, 238 pp.

" This is a German reprint of Thomas Norton's ' Ordinal of Alchemy,' A.D. 1618. It contains seven fine alchemical plates after De Bey, which were not published in the former editions." (Gardner, " Bibl. Rosa.," No. 354.)

The dedication, which is very neatly expressed, is dated at Frankfurt-on-Maine, January 1618. To " Dn. Joanni Hartmanno Beyero," Doctor of Medicine, physician in ordinary to the " Imperial Republic " of Frankfurt, and a privy councillor. Maier offers the precious treatises—now put by him into a Latin dress—to his friend, the most learned and kindly, the very glory of Frankfurt, whose princes and magnates are the glory of Germany—a golden Tripod. He doubts not that such an offering will further their true friendship and concord, and that he will not repent of his labour in translating the treatises into the common language of Europe.—*Vale*. Three epigrammatic poems by Maier precede the three treatises.

The figures are very curious. The first, at page 12, is labelled " Mirabilis Naturæ," a square in a circle. About the square are the words, "Aer, Ignis, Aqua, Terra"; in the

outer circle, the signs of the Zodiac. The twelve keys have
twelve illustrative cuts. Some are curious. That of the
sixth key represents the marriage ceremony—the alchemistic union of Sol et Luna. Fire burns in a furnace at the
masculine side ; water is being poured into a retort at the
feminine side. The seventh key represents Chaos, out of
which come " Spring, Summer, Autumn, Winter"—a square
with a triangle in the centre. In the latter appears the
word "aqua," and beneath it, in the square, " Sal philosophorum." The eleventh key represents the marriage of
Orpheus and Eurydice. They are seated on lions, which
are mouthing each other. Each person holds a heart, out
of which springs a sun and moon. A number of cubs seem
to be enjoying the rush of liquid issuing from the female
lion.

Basil Valentine is referred to in the present work
under the title " Symbolum." See also Waite's " Lives," p.
120, *et seq.* ; Ferguson's " Bib. Chemica," *in voce.* Dissertation on the " 12 Keys," in South's " Suggestive Enquiry,"
p. 474, *et seq.*

Thomas Norton.—See Waite's " Lives," p. 130, *et seq.*
The " first publication of the ' Ordinal' was in the Latin
translation by Michael Mair. . . In his book ' Symbola
Aureæ Mensæ,' printed in the previous year, he speaks of it
being still ' uneditus,' but ' to be published shortly by us.'
It was afterwards published by Ashmole ; 4to ; Lon. 1652.
See Ferguson, *in voce*; Wood's "Athenæ," iv. 359.

" Testamentum Cremeri." Cremer is said to have been
Abbot of Westminster in the fourteenth century. Dis-
satisfied with the results of his alchemical labours, he went
to visit Lullius at Milan, in 1330, and learned part of the
mystery from him. Lullius came to London, and worked
with Cremer. They supplied Edward III. with gold, who
is said to have used it against France. The whole story is

more than doubtful, and the "Testament" has been regarded as spurious. This document was also first printed by Maier in this collection.[1]

"All wisdom is from God. He who loves wisdom, let him ask of God, and he will receive it. All is open to God ; with Him is the treasury of wisdom ; from Him, by Him, and in Him are all things. It has willed God to illumine my spirit by His grace, to lead me in the way of truth, to whom be all praise, who reigns 'in excelsis' for ever and ever.—Amen."

Cremer has also a prayer for God's blessing upon the work in the fire about to be kindled—"May the most merciful God sanctify all by His blessing, granting perfection to the human race." Five verses of a Latin hymn follow. We have next a prescription for "aqua viva." It is founded on "bonum vinum clareti," strong and pure, to which are added various ingredients—petroleum, sulphur, arsenic, willow ashes. To be kept tightly closed. Another, and rather a strange preparation, is "aqua est distillanda" —"bis ex urina juvenis octodecim annorum non polluti." This ingredient is to be obtained after the first sleep, for three or four nights ; to be then left for some time in a stone dish, lime and vinegar being added ; the whole then placed in an alembic—this process to be continued for some time. A portrait is given of Cremer by Ashmole.[2]

[1] See Waite's "Lives," p. 83, *et seq.* ; Ferguson's "Bibl. Chem.," *in voce.*
[2] See his "Theatrum Chemicum Brittanicum," 1652, pp. 213, 465-67.

THEMIS AUREA, hoc est, de Legibus Fraternitatis R.C. Tractatus. Quo earum cum rei veritate convenientia, utilitatis publica et privata, nec non causa necessaria, evolvuntur et demonstrantur. Authore Michaele Maiero Imperialis Consist. Comite, Equite, Exempt. Phil. et Med. D. &c.

[Woodcut of angels' heads blowing a volcano ; on a surrounding circle the motto, "Adversis clarius ardeo."] Francoforti, Typis Nicholai Hoffmanni. sumptibus Lucæ Iennis, 1618 ; 8vo ; pp. 192.
—BRITISH MUSEUM.

THEMIS AUREA, The Laws of the Fraternity of the Rosie Cross. Written in Latin by Count Michael Maierus, and now in English for the Information of those who seek after the knowledge of that Honourable and Mysterious Society of wise and renowned Philosophers. Quæ non fecimus ipsi vix ea nostra voco. Whereto is annexed an Epistle to the Fraternity in Latin from some here in England. London : Printed for N. Brooke at the Angel in Cornhill, 1656. 32o.

Dedication, 3 pp. ; preface, 3 pp. ; Latin letter, 22 pp. ; work, 136 pp. List of books sold by Brooke follows in 8 pp. ; one cut, anagram, p. 115 ; also with "Silentio" ; 8vo ; pp. 192; 1624. (Latin.) "Eliza Berkley" on leaf. —UNIVERSITY OF ABERDEEN.

The translation is dedicated to " the most excellently accomplish't, The only Philosopher in the present age : The Honoured, Noble, Learned, Elias Ashmole, Esq., by

N. L., T. S., and H. S., who desire so to aquit ourselves as that you may have no cause to repent of those kindnesses and respects wherewith you have or shall honour your servants," &c. In 1651, Ashmole "began to learn seal graving, casting in sand, and goldsmith's work," living in the "Blackfryars in London," "at which time he, being very knowing in chymistry, and accounted a great Rosy Crucian, Will. Backhouse of Swallowfield, in Berks, Esq.," communicated to him "several secrets in that faculty, which ever after caused Ashmole to call him father. . . On the 10th of March 1652, his father, Backhouse, opened himself very freely to him the secret." Afterwards Backhouse, thinking himself dying, told him further secrets of the society. Backhouse became a commoner of Christ Church, Oxford, at the age of seventeen, in 1610; "left it without a degree, and at length, settling on his patrimony, became a most renowned chymist, Rosicrucian," &c. He published translations of several ancient treatises on mystic alchemy (Wood, "Athenæ Oxon.," iv. 355-6; iii. 576-7). We have here what may be looked upon as a succession of three Rosicrucians—Maier and Fludd the first; Backhouse the second; Ashmole the third. The dedication to Ashmole was thus proper and suitable. It is followed by "The Preface," in three pages, "to the Courteous Reader." It commences with the old mystic tale, relating that the "goddess Themis, after the Deluge, being asked of Deucalion and Pyrrha how mankind, swept away with the overflowing of the Waters, should again be restored and multiplied," commanded "them to throw over their heads the Bones of their Great Mother, the which Oracle they rightly interpreted concerning the Stones of the Earth." Deucalion and his wife Pyrrha "are the Gabritius and Beia, the Sun and Moon, which two, by projection of their Specific Stones, can multiply even to a thousand." Pyrrha is ruddy, though outwardly white, and Deucalion is a lion spiritually. He is "so cruel to his wife that he kills her, and then he wraps her with his bloody mantle." Few understand this Oracle, since Moses apprehends it to be only a history, "and now the Title is vindicated, viz., why we call it the Golden Themis." Following the preface is an address to the true Philosophers, the brothers of the R.C., "S.P.D. Theod. verax. Theophil. Cælnatus." The work follows, and with it the pagination begins. It is divided into twenty chapters. The first treats of all laws, and resolves the question who Themis is, "feigned by the poets to be the Daughter of Heaven and Earth, the Sister of Saturn, and Aunt to Jupiter." Though there "never was upon the face of the earth any such Themis, yet she represents the true Idea of Justice, and the universal Notion of Vertue." The next chapter shows that the "Laws which the Founder of this Fraternity prescribed to the R.C." to be "all good and just." These are six:—The profession of medicine and cures to be made gratis. That no special "habit" is necessary. A yearly meeting upon the Day C. Every brother to choose his successor. That the word R.C. shall be their seal, character, and cognisance. And, lastly, that the society should be concealed an hundred years. "Our author of these laws is namelesse, but yet worthy of credit, unknown to the vulgar, but well known to his own society."

In regard to the Brethren, they do not repent of their condition, being servants to the King of kings. "Religion with them is in greater esteem than anything in the world." In the Book "M," the brethren, "as in a glass, clearly see the Anatomy and Idea of the Universe. The different laws of the Society are then in the next chapter more fully gone into. The brethren, though not in a measure highly educated, yet "compound that medicine which they administer, it being, as it were, the marrow of the great world." It is the fire of Prometheus, which he stole from the Sun. But a fourfold fire is required to bring this medicine to perfection. Like Galen, the Brethren have "variety of medicines, some called Kings, some Princes, some Nobles, and others Knights." "We hold that there is a natural vertue and certain predestination flowing from the influence of heavenly bodies." "And Avicenna perhaps meant thus much—a select company of choice soldiers have a great advantage over a confused multitude." Is it not a rare society of men who are injurious to none, but seek the good and happiness of all, giving to each person what appertains to him? There are many abuses in medicine, long bills of ostentation, " when a few choice simples might do the cure." Medicines with great titles may be in great esteem, "but others of lesser price are far above them in excellence and worth." Chemists wrongly scorn the use of vegetable and " Galenical compositions," which yet may be useful " in proper cases." Both parties " are swayed more by Fancy than Reason." Many physicians have insufferable vices, "from which the Fraternity of R.C. is free." Like " that monster Aristotle, who (as it is reported), was so spightful to his master Plato, that he caused many of his works to be burned that he might shine brighter," many possess this evil spirit of Malice and Hatred. " In medicine, such practices are more dangerous." On the other hand, the Brethren are neither emulous nor arrogant, " but delight in instructing one another in mysteries." But their cure is not at the command of all. When called, they need not appear unless they choose. Cardan blasphemously subjects God Himself to fatal necessity, but " we hold that God is a free agent, omnipotent—He can do whatever He pleaseth; He hath made Nature His handmaid." The birth and original of vice " proceeds from the corrupted nature of fallen man."

The Brethren " do use only lauful and natural remedies." Isaiah used the simple application of Figs to the Jewish King. One, " with the application of one simple, took away the raging pain of an ulcerated cancer." This happened at Wetzlar. God has not placed so many lights in the heavens, for no purpose " but that Vegetables, Mineralls, and Animals do receive their occult Qualities from them." The Brethren " apply themselves only to the study of

Natural Magic." This is "the highest, most absolute, and divinest knowledge of Natural Philosophy." But we are to beware lest "this noble science," degenerating, becomes Diabolical. Though the Brethren do not use one and the same habit, yet "they are always civilly clad." They have also thought it expedient to meet once a year in a certain place. Thus the "Brethren of the R.C. in Germany meet for a good end—to vindicate abused Nature, to settle Truth in her power, and chiefly that they may with one accord return thanks to God for revealing such mysteries to them. We cannot set down the places where they meet, neither the time. I have sometimes observed Olympick Houses not far from a river, and known a city which we think is called S. Spiritus—I meane Helicon, or Parnassus, in which Pegasus opened a spring of overflowing water, wherein Diana wash'd her selfe, to whom Venus was handmaid, and Saturne gentleman usher. This will sufficiently instruct an Intelligent reader, but more confound the ignorant." The Brethren are but mortals, they will cease to be. As in Egypt, the sons did not merely inherit their father's estate, but also his daily employment. So amid the Philosophers, there were always sons of Philosophers. The Brethren wish their mysteries only to be revealed to those whom God may enlighten ; so they must be "men of approved parts, and very vertuous." A succession is most necessary. In this way all ancient knowledge has been preserved, as "the cabalystical art was found out, and by word of mouth communicated." The Heathen Colleges were composed of the "picke of the most able, and they were few." So is the custom in the Fraternity of the R.C.

Hieroglyphics were anciently signs and characters of deep knowledge. "The characters are R.C., which they use that they may not be without Name, and every one, according to his capacity, may put an interpretation upon the letters, as soon as their first writing come forth ; shortly after they were called Rosie Crucians, for R. may stand for Roses, and C. for Cross, which appellation yet remains,

although the Brethren have declared that thereby they
symbolically mean the name of their first Author." Each
order has its " Formalities and coat of armis or Emblemne.
The Rhodians have the double cross, they of Burgundy the
golden fleece, &c. So R.C. cover mysteries. R. signifies
Pegasus, C. Iulium, if you look not to the letter, but right
interpretation "—" is not this a claw of a rosy lion—a drop
of Hippocrene ? " " To live amidst Roses and under a
Crosse are contrary things—joy and sorrow." An anagram
is given (p. 115).

By the will of the first author, the Fraternity was to be
concealed for one hundred years, hoping that period " would
give the world time to lay aside their vanities, folly, and
madnesse." The dates are added. The detection of the
Fraternity did increase the word's glory. By Hercules is
understood " a laborious and skilfull philosopher, by Anteus
the subject to be wrought upon." Osiris, about to travel
into India, consulted with Prometheus, " did joyn Mercury
as a governor, and Hercules as President of the Provinces,
by whose direction and his own industry he always accomplished his end. He used Vulcan's shop, the golden house
where Apis is fed and nourished." So the Brethren " have
overcome Anteus, they have sufficiently declared their
Herculean strength, the wit of Mercury, and the Providence of Prometheus."

The Book " M " contains " the perfection of all the Arts,
beginning with the Heavens, and descending to lower
Sciences." " Lastly, the Brethren have a secret of incredible Vertue, by which they can give Piety, justice, and
truth the upperhand in any person whom they effect, and
suppress the opposite vices." Absurd fables have been
spoken about the Brethren. All in the world seek to carry
out their own intentions. Let " Rome, therefore, that
whore of Babylon, return into the right way, so may a
reformation be produced, and piety and religion shall
flourish." But such Reformations belong to God. The
Brethren pray for it, they try to enlighten the under-

standing, but God alone can change the will. There is no confusion amongst the Brethren, they "have alwaies had one amongst them as chiefe and governor, to whom they are obedient." "They have the true Astronomy, the true Physics, Mathematicks, Medicine, and Chymistry, by which they are able to produce rare and wonderful effects; they are very laborious, frugall, temperate, secret, true ; lastly, make it their business to be profitable and beneficial to all men, of whom, when we have spoken the highest commendations, we must confess our insufficiency to reach their worth. Finis."

In the "Themis," the Brethren of the Rosy Cross appear merely as specially amiable and virtuous medical practitioners, who, having either by tradition inherited, or by devotion and a peculiar astrology, discovered certain medicines, are ready to treat the diseased with these, gratis, out of love to mankind. They, too, appear as possessing a certain strength of moral virtue, a natural religion, which makes men whom they counsel and befriend noble and virtuous. In short, they are merely a society of men, "very laborious, frugall, temperate, secret, true."

The story of Christian Rosencreutz, at least the history of his burial, discovery, and the alleged dates of the founding of the society, are treated as facts. There may be some reason to suppose these in a measure correct. The " Book M " may be either " Meus," or " Mundus," the place " C," where the house of S. Spiritus is existent " Corpus." [1]

---

[1] See Waite, " Real Hist. of the Rosicrucians," p. 271-2 ; Wood, "Athenæ Oxon.," iii. 724. Here it is said that Ashmole " hath utterly forgotten" who N.L., T.S., H.S., who sign the English Dedication to him, " are."

MICHAELIS MAJERI VIATORIUM, hoc est, De Montibus Planetarum Septem seu Metallorum ; Tractatus
tam utilis, quam perspicuus, quo, ut Indice Mercuriali
in triviis, vel Ariadneo filo in Labyrintho, seu
Cynosura in Oceano Chymicorum errorum immenso,
quilibet rationalis, veritatis amans, ad illum, qui in
montibus sese abdidit DE Rubea-petra Alexicacum
omnibus Medicis desideratum, investigandum, uti,
poterit. Oppenheimii Ex typographia Hieronymi
Galleri, Sumptibus Joh. Theodori de Bry. MDCXVIII.

The title-page is surrounded by a pictured border. At the top is
a figure of Maier seated with a compass-box in his left hand—the
picture more pleasing than the larger engraving. On the outer side
are three figures of Sol, Luna, Mars ; on the left, four figures of
Mercury, Saturn, Jupiter, Venus ; at the bottom, a scene of Land
and Water. Seven symbolic engravings in text ; 4to ; epigramma
authoris, 1 p. ; dedication, 2 pp. ; prefatio, 6 pp. ; whole work, 136
pp. ; A³-S. —AUTHOR'S LIBRARY.

The same, " Rothomagi Sumpt. Ioannis Berthelin, in Aræ Palatij,
anno MDCLI." 8vo ; 224 pp. ; engraved title included ; seven
engravings ; vignette.   —FERGUSON'S " BIBL. CHEM."
                              — L. DE FRESNOY'S LIST.
                              —GARDNER, 356.

The " Epigramma Authoris," on the back of the title-
page, compares the labours of chemists with those who
vainly sought to trace the Labyrinth before Ariadne gave
the clue. The author is to supply a " Viatorium " for those
who seek to scale the heavens, to know the mystery of the
planets and their metallic symbols.

The dedication is given to Christian, Prince of Anhalt

and relates to the "opusculum," following the result of the author's experience and observation, "ars longa, vita brevis, judicium difficile." He speaks of favours received from the Prince—whom with his consort and family he commends to the care of God. The dedication is from Frankfurt, September 1618.

The Preface to the Reader follows. It commences with a reference to the most beautiful allegory—that in the second book of Ovid's " Metamorphosis "—the transformation of Battus to a Touchstone. Battus was sensible to bribery. He took the first bribe :—

> " ' Go, stranger,' cries the clown, securely on,
>   This stone shall sooner tell, and shows a stone ;

yet ready to tell, for a further bribe, what he had concealed :—

> " ' Neighbour, hast thou seen a stray
>   Of bullocks and of heifers pass this way?'
>
>   The peasant quick replies, ' You'll find them there,
>   In yon dark vale, and in the vale they were—
>   The double bribe had his false heart beguil'd.
>
>   Then to a touchstone turns the faithless spy."

What was understood by the flock has been abundantly shown, " Utpote, Hieroglyphicis Ægypti, Græcis." The oxen were the material philosophic, which from the Mount of Mercury had been stolen. The stories of Narcissus and of Echo have also an arcane reference. The Minotaur in the Labyrinth is also " materia philosophica " : —

> " The Cretan Labyrinth of old,
>   With wand'ring ways and many a winding fold
>   Involv'd the weary Feet, without redress,
>   In a round Error, which deny'd recess."

So says Virgil. Here were detained the captives, having no guide to lead them out of their perplexity. The story of Dædalus is also referred to. Now we have a crowd of would-be philosophers who vainly attempt by a thousand efforts to solve the difficulty, to give an exit from the Labyrinth. But it is necessary to take counsel with Nature. So it is hoped that a way may be found to ascend the planetary mountains, and, using the true glass, see through the many errors which have been made. Thus will those who have been wandering on the mountains, seeking for, but not knowing, the true " materia philosophica," find the clue of Ariadne, and, like Theseus, slay the Minotaur.

The work itself commences with the story from Tacitus of Cecilius Bassus, who perverted a dream he had into a story, which he went to Rome to tell Nero, that on his estates there had been discovered an immense cavern, containing a vast mass of gold, in ingots and bars, hidden there from the most ancient times. He suggested that Dido the Phœnician, when he fled from Tyre and founded Carthage, had secreted this treasure. Nero rather hastily sent persons to take away the supposed spoil. Three-oared galleys and chosen mariners were employed to facilitate despatch. Alas! the hoped-for riches became the cause of public poverty. Bassus was deceived, and after efforts in excavations, again and again renewed, he is said to have suffered a voluntary death. Maier applies this story " in chymicis operibus." Many, perhaps with good intentions, yet as in a dream, attempt to gain the portal, but, being ignorant of the method, are helpless and unsuccessful.

The treatise then divides itself into seven chapters— the first, " De Monte Mercurii." Referring back to the story of Battus, he applies it to the nature of Mercury, a metal not mallable, yet cohesive. Then, in three sub-divisions, its relation to gold, to the " Tincture," and to the " Medicine " is discussed. Chapter II. is " De Monte Saturni." By Saturn we do not understand here either the planet " illum Mundi Supremum," nor the God of that name, but a metallic substance—that is, Lead. It is placed next to Mercury, " cum et in artis philosophicæ et naturæ operatione hac serie illum sequatur, testantibus Philosophis et ipsius rei experimentis." Under three heads, as before, the relation of " Saturn," or lead, to the gold, to the

" Tincture," and to the " Medicine " is detailed. The third chapter is " De Monte Jovis "—the greatest of the gods, elevated between Saturn and Mars. Here the term refers to the next metal—Tin. " Jupiter planeta calidus et humidus . . . an earundem qualitatem et virium sit metallum ejus nominis." Tin is precious, " ad coagulationem in metallum perfectum, argentum ac aurum." Then its relation to the " Tincture" and the " Medicine" follow. At p. 66 is the plate, " Idolum Jovis," and a curious and not particularly edifying story told of Agathocles, Tyrant of Sicily, who formed an image of Jupiter out of a golden basin " previously used for the purposes of nature." He then rebuked the folly of those who had contemned him for his obscure birth. As he is said to have been a *potter* to trade, the comparison was not inapplicable. The story is told to rebuke those who might suppose that this metal was despicable. The next is " De Monte Veneris." Venus stands for as most beautiful in body. Copper is the metal. Yet Janus, like brass, is under her protection. Tubal Cain was, as we read in holy writ, the first who dug in the earth for metals, brought them to light, and used them in various works. So in Solomon's Temple, next to gold, the works of fine brass held place. So at Corinth, brass excelled and held the place of honour. The heads are as before :—Usu ad aurum de usu ad Tincturam." This is to be better understood by the figure given—that of the anatomy of the Chameleon. Democritus, " ex Abdera oriundus," coming to Egypt, the Mother of all the Sciences, laughing at much that the philosophers and priests told him, was, however, eager to know the cause of the folly and vanity of men. The anatomy of man and animals became his study. The Chameleon and the Crocodile, found in Egypt, attracted his close attention. The Chameleon, in its changes of black, green, red, and other colours, has been a source of deep philosophic study. Democritus is said to have been also in correspondence with Hippocrates " de usu Medicinam." The next is " De Monte Martis," a metal of a hard nature—Iron. The three uses follow. At page 92 is a cut representing the story of Mucius Scævola, who appears in the act of stabbing the secretary of King Porsenna, whom he mistook for the King. A story is also added of Barbarossa and Saladin. Reference is also made "usu ad Medicinam" to the value of iron in chalybeate wells and in embrocation and syrups, also in a dry state of powder. The effect is astringent. Chapter sixth is "De Monte Luna"—Silver. Our journey is through the more imperfect to the perfect. This is the method in Nature. Though much inferior, yet still silver has something of the nature of gold. Reference is made to the experiments at Zellarfeld. "Usu, seu coagulatione Lunæ in Aurum"—then "ad tincturam." Under this head we have a cut representing "Terrarum orbis circumscriptio," representing in front a ship in full sail, one man appearing on board, behind a king on apparently a small shoal or island, and then two birds, probably eagles, flying in opposite directions, referring to a Delphian story of Jupiter sending off two eagles in order to ascertain where lay the centre of the earth. They returned back and arrived together at Delphi, which was thus proved to be the centre. The man in the ship is Magellan, who circumnavigated the globe, proving its rotundity. These are but figures of the sun and moon in their journeys. "Duo sunt lapides principales, albus et rubeus mirabilis naturæ."

The seventh and last section is "De Monte Solis." The medicine procured here is the noblest of all—all life, all action in chemistry flow from this. Here is the complete arcana. All metals, minerals and "lapides" are generated, nourished, increased, by the virtue and spirit of Sol. Then the power of dew, rain, snow, all flow from this influence. Vapours and mists descend, and cold, congealing, ascends. "So as the seed of the wheat is in the wheat, so the seed of the gold lies in the gold." The solution of gold is then treated of. In regard to this, four opinions are given, and four answers to them are noted. The woodcut is

entitled " Hic est Leo hospes Hominis, hic est Homo medicus Leonis," and represents a man sitting at the foot of a
tree, a lion before him holding in his mouth a prey, which
he offers to the man. In the forefront is a circular theatre,
in which a man is leading round a lion by a rope. The
lion seems quite tame.

It is an old Roman story of the man who, for his
wickedness, fled into the wood, where a huge lion lay, but
which allowed itself to be treated by the man for a torn
foot. The lion offering its foot to the man, he took it in
his hand and extracted the thorn. The lion thereafter
becoming even more friendly, when he had caught a prey
brought part to the man for his own use. But at last the
lion was captured, and, being remarkable for size, was sent
to Rome. The man soon after also arrived there. The lion
refused to attack him in the arena, but showed himself as
before gentle and quiet. Both were released—the people
crying, " The man is the doctor of the lion, and the lion the
provider for the man." This also has, no doubt, an arcane
meaning. A very great medicine is to be had, " usu auri."
" Aurum potabile " was well known to the ancient philosophers. Did not Moses know this secret when he dissolved
the remains of the golden calf and made the Israelites
drink their god.

May God, the Greatest and the Best, grant to all those
of good will, and who are legitimate sons of the art, the use
of the golden Nepenthes, which will drive away grief and
sorrow, so that, with joy and quietness of mind, they may
give thanks to God for ever and for ever.

VERUM INVENTUM, Hoc est, Munera Germaniæ, ab ipsa primitus reperta (non ex vino, ut calumniator quidam scoptice invehit, sed vi animi et corporis) et reliquo Orbi communicata, quæ tanta sunt, ut plæraque eorum mutationem Mundo singularem attullerint, universa longe utilissima extiterint, Tractatu peculiari evoluta et tradita. Authore Michaele Maiero, comite Imperialis Consistorii, Equite, Exempto, Phil. et Med. D. P. C. olim Aulico Cæsar. nunc illustriss. Princip. ac Dn. Mauritii. Hassiæ Landg. avii, &c. Archiatro. anno 1619. Francofurti, Typis Nicolai Hoffmanni, sumpibus Lucæ Iennis.

Vignette of a burning mountain ; flames and a star intermingled ; on vignette, motto—"Adversis clarius ardet" ; 8vo ; on back of title-page, Ioannis Owenus Britannus Epigramm. 18. lib. i.

Si latet in vino verum, ut proverbia dicunt
Invenit verum Teuto, vel inveniet
Responsio authoris.
Sis vates, fatuusve licet, verum Owene dicis
Invenit verum Teuto, sed absque mero.

Dedication to the Town Counsellors of the free and imperial City [Argentinensis], dated at Frankfurt, Sep. 1618. Preface to the Reader follows, with a number of poetical pieces and epigrams, with quotations from Tacitus and Florus ; 250 pp.
—ADVOCATES' LIBRARY, Edinburgh.

The " Verum Inventum " is divided into six parts or chapters. The first chapter is, " De primo vero Universali Politico." It treats of the earliest state of Germany, of its connection with the Romans, Charlemagne, the gift of Germany to the Emperor by the Pope, " cuius non erat."

The second chapter continues the history, "Caroli magni stirpe mascula extincta," the Saxons and the Othos. The third chapter speaks of the nature of the Imperial prerogative, " præ aliis regnis, quæ dignitas et quæ utilitas." The fourth chapter is about the German inventions in the art of war, warlike machines and implements. Albertus Magnus, Bertholdus Schwartz, and other inventors are spoken of. Here we have the first glimpse of the chemic, philosophic stone which Adam brought out of Paradise, and carried about with him wherever he went, and which is "in te, in me, et in quolibet alio," as Morien relates. The account of the invention of gunpowder, or a denotating powder devised by Swartz, follows, made of sulphur, charcoal, and salt. This " pulveris Pyrii" was prefigured by the flames of Pluto, and the natural flames of Hecla, Ætna, and Vesuvius. The Germans also used " ballistæ," such as described by Ovid. These threw huge stones, and, it is believed, were first used by the Phœnicians. The testudo also was known. The vase or box of Pandora, which dispersed good and evil throughout the world, was but a picture of the many German inventions. The fifth chapter treats of early literary works in Germany. Writing was brought from Egypt and Chaldea to the Phœnicians, thence to the Greeks, to Spain and Gaul, from the Greeks to the Romans, and from the Romans to Germany. By-and-by, a great and valuable number of manuscripts were stored up in the libraries of Heidelberg and other cities. The invention of printing was German, and John Gutenberg, anno 1440, issued volumes which may be seen in the University Library of Basle. Chinese printing is also referred to. The sixth chapter treats of the Theological gifts of Germany, referring to the " purificatio doctrinæ Theologicæ," for which Germany is famous throughout the whole world. Buchanan's lines on the Church of Rome are quoted—" Non ego Romulea miror quod pastor in urbe," &c. The history of the Pontifex Maximus, the Flamens, the Vestals, the Augurs, &c., as illustrating the origin of the Roman ecclesiastical power, is related. Pope Gregory appears on the scene with the two keys and the lightnings of excommunication and indulgences. The great amount of money raised for the papal treasury is incredible. Wicklif and John of Hus are referred to. The Turks, Jews, even the heathens, have served their faiths better than Christians have done. Then came Savonarola, to be succeeded by Luther. "Doctor Martinus Lutherus, Saxo," whose story is detailed, the Roman party condemned, particularly on the point of transubstantiation, and a return to the teaching of Christ, the Apostles, and the primitive Church upheld— the use of lustral water, borrowed from the Egyptians, and the use of extreme unction, the number of seven in the Sacraments held, "non est credibile," but the means in past times of extortion — riches, fields, and all kinds of gifts being taken from princes, rich men, and kingdoms. The treatment by the popes of the German kings and princes is also referred to. The Roman tyranny is derived from the power of Lucifer and Diabolus. "Verbum Christi scriptum nobis sufficit ad salutem," so we hope that, founded on the adamantine rock of the word of God, and joined together in the truth, we are safe against waters, fires, temporal injuries, all cemented together, "verum Inventum a Germanis," we will be preserved in all Christian peace and concord, giving to God the Tri-une glory and praise for ever and ever.

The next chapter treats of the "Invention" of the Germans "in Medicina."

As "ex montanis Helvetiorum" the Evangelic doctrine proceeded, so also in regard to medicine, the voice of the teacher proclaims "purifactio a fæcibus humanis" in medical practice. Philip Bombast — Paracelsus — loosed the chains of ignorance and arose a teacher both in the works of chemistry and in Experimental Medicine. There are in Germany, Gaul, Italy, England, Scotland, Poland, Spain, and elsewhere, even in Muscovy, Sweden, and Denmark,

I

many thousands of " Medici " who are now profiting by his labours. He was a fitting successor of Albertus Magnus. His epitaph at Saltzburg is given by Maier (p. 205). He not only cured leprosy, gout, and dropsy, but gave all his goods to the poor. The state of medicine in Italy and the connection of the popes with it is then referred to.

The saying of Apollo in the Ovid may be applied to Paracelsus :—

> " Inventum Medicina meum est, opifexque per orbem
> Dicor et herbarum subjecta potentia nobis."

The last division is of the German inventions, " in Chymia." This section occupies thirty pages. Enough has been said of German invention or discoveries to prove that little can be added by others to what has been done in that country. Reference is made at once to the " Silentio" and the " Themis." Undoubtedly singular gifts have been bestowed by learned and God-illuminated men.

From very ancient times it has been whispered that a medicine exists which not only cures all the ills of the flesh, but can transmute into gold other metals. The matter has been set forth, and the thirty-six arguments of the adversary repelled in " Symbolis nostris Aureæ Mensæ," where also the truth is declared from the writings of persons of twelve different nations *ad nauseam.*

Are then the Brothers of the R.C., who certainly must exist, to be preferred in knowledge to the vulgar alchemists? Believing that they have this divine art for the last 200 years, having received it from their founder; that they themselves deserve the reverence of all men; that their society is the very asylum of piety ; that in it are gathered together all virtue, temperance, strictness, chastity ; that they do not give themselves up to ease, but to the assistance of humanity. If such men have this art, it must indeed be the very perfection of science. Think what Plato paid for the three Pythagoric books - ten thousand denarii—that he might increase his knowledge. It is true that books, being now printed, do not fetch such prices, but knowledge, which

in a short time will change, and perfect metals, which by
nature take ages to mature, must be of the greatest value.
To say that such a thing is impossible or improper is, indeed, contrary to the Word of God in holy Scripture, as it
is to say that God and man are two contraries. For it is
quite evident that Moses was not ignorant of "chymia"
when he caused the golden calf to become powder, and
changed it into golden water, of which the Israelites had to
drink. Avicenna has truly said that unless a grain of
wheat fall into the earth it cannot multiply; so if we do not
see gold and silver, then we need not believe in the art, "sed
quia video, scio, quod sit vera." Yes! caluminators should
be severely punished, a doctrine shown to be true from the
case of Miriam and from the writings of St Jerome, St
Gregory, Origen, St Bernard.

Some, indeed, have said that the brethren of the R.C.
exist nowhere, but are fictitious phantasms of the German
brain merely. We have already shown this to be false.
In the twelfth book, the "Symbolis Aureæ Mensæ," we have
given proofs to the contrary.

In conclusion, it is to be judged that all men hold in
the highest esteem such benefits, and by a good life, temperate and gentle, find a way to all that is good. The
Papists blame Dr Luther for all the tumults and rebellions
made by the Anabaptists of Munster, so as falsely might
the enemies of the order blame it for the folly of its
imitators. The Ephesian idolators brought many crimes
against St Paul in order to cause a seditious rising; so now
these brethren are blamed for not putting instruction in the
first place, but they only act as the apostles did who received from God the power of healing. Without detracting
from the achievements of other nations, a high place must
be given to the German nation for accomplishments in all
the liberal arts, in the art of war and of navigation. Maier
concludes with an eulogy of the magnificence of the German
princes and nobles, their splendid castles, the riches of the
country in fields, woods, rivers, horses, soldiers—cavalry as

well as infantry—so that only the army of Xerxes might be considered superior. They have been in all parts of Europe redoubtable in war. Only a few years ago 200,000 were in Belgium, France, and Hungary, such is the populousness of Germany. May it please the Great Arbiter of peoples and of kingdoms that Germany may ever flourish, and that the other Christian kingdoms living in peace may give no occasion for the increase of the Turkish tyranny, but gladly bear the easy yoke of Christianity.

At the back of page 249 :—" Francofurti ad Mænum Nicolai Hoffmanni, Sumptibus Lucæ Jennis"; then the same vignette as on the title page—" Anno MDCXIX."

TRACTATUS DE VOLUCRI ARBOREA, absque Patre et Matre, in Insulis ORCHADVM, forma Ansercul-orum proveniente, seu De ortu Miraculoso potius, quam naturali Vegetabilium, animalium, hominum et supranaturalium quorundam. Quo causæ illius et horum inquiruntur, et demonstrantur. Authore Michaele Maiero, Comite Imperialis Consistorii, Equite, Exempto, Phil. & Med. D. P. C. olim Aulico Cæsar. nunc illustriss Princip. ac Dn. Mauritii. Hassiæ Landgravij., &c., Archiatro. Francofurti, Typis Nicolai Hoffmanni, Sumptibus Lucæ Iennis. Anno MDCXIX.

8vo ; dedication, 1 p. ; prefatio, 4 pp. ; epigramma authoris, 2 pp. ; series capitum, 4 pp. ; work, p. 23-180.
—AUTHOR'S LIBRARY.

Several works by Maier are of a more popular nature than the " Arcana " or the " Symbola." This is one of them. It may be called a " Little Book of Nature's Marvels," or, more correctly, of marvels contrary to Nature, for not only does it contain an account of the wonderful Tree-bird, but also of the Tartarian Lamb, the Tree of Dragon's Blood, the Phœnix, the Green Boys seen in England, the ancient Greek monsters, the Incubi et Succubi, the Lycanthropes, Lamiæ, Satyrs, and other wonders. It is a delightfully interesting book, and if it had been translated into English, would have circulated far more widely than the " Lusus Serius." The dedication is on the back of the title-pages, and is made to the author's friend, Dominus Johannes Hardtmuthus, ab Hutten, and a councillor of Wirtemberg.

The preface to the reader follows. The wonderful ways of Nature, says the author, are seen in the many, yet sometimes strange and uncommon, works of God. The strange things ought not to be considered monstrous or regarded as a sort of error in Nature—mere matters for amusement, and even laughter. All things made by God should command respect. Children, who sometimes amuse us, we ought to respect, for by-and-by they will be soldiers and politicians. No mother would like her children to be subjects of ridicule ; so Nature, the mother of all, when she shows us strange, infrequent, and uncommon sights, asks for our respect, if not admiration.

Thus the author is to tell us the story of the wonderful birds which have their birth in the Orkney Islands. A certain Scot, Doctor of Medicine, having procured over fifty of these creatures, has demonstrated to us their rare and wonderful nature, so strange that the author has prepared this tract to give an account of them. They are to be to us emblems of the power and knowledge of God, who Himself was born into the world without a human father through a divine mother, and became the Mediator between God and man, so that by Him our poor, weak hearts are lifted up to the contemplation of the Greatest and the Best.

Max Muller and others have considered this comparison " blasphemous," but it is not so, and never was meant to be so. Just as the figure of the fish in the Catacombs taught the early Christian the fact of baptism, and as circumcision was the token of an older covenant, so here, although now we know the comparison to be false, it was to the writer and others a subject of believing inquiry, and an illustration from Nature of a great fact.

An epigram by the author follows, then the contents of the sixteen chapters.

The introductory chapter shows us that Nature is not eternal, but created by God in time, and the smallest works in Nature give a testimony to the power of God to man, who himself is but a part of Nature. Proclus, and other

" Ethnics," are wrong in supposing the world to be eternal, for the human intellect cannot grasp such an idea. Nature is indeed the vicar of God, and the conservator of His power. Wonderful thought, how that order was brought out of chaos ! The author then breaks forth into an ascription of praise to God in His glorious, unerring providence and clemency, who from nothing has brought forth things rare and beautiful, light from darkness, the Earth, the Heavens, the Sun, Moon, and Stars. Even these sing aloud the hymn of creation, redemption, and sanctification. Even the wisest of men have been pleased to write concerning the smallest works of and objects in Nature—Marcion the Greek on the radish, Cato on the cabbage, others on the nettle, the broom, and the chameleon. Pythagoras is said to have written on the onion ; others have thought midges, ants, bees, even turnips, not beneath their notice. All are in their several places worthy of Nature, their mother.

The curious story of the Barnacle geese can be traced as far back as the twelfth century. Giraldus Cambrensis, in his " Topographia Hiberniæ," relates it thus :—These birds " are produced from fir timber tossed into the sea, and are at first sight like gum. Afterwards they hang down by their beaks as from a seaweed attached to the timber, surrounded by shells in order to grow more freely. Having thus, in process of time, been clothed with a strong coat of feathers, they either fall into the water or fly freely away into the air. They derive their food and growth from the sap of the wood, or the sea, by a secret and most wonderful process of alimentation. I have frequently, with my own eyes, seen more than a thousand of these small bodies of birds, hanging down on the seashore from one piece of timber, enclosed in shells, and already formed."

Hector Boece (1465-1536), author of the " History of Scotland," translated by Bellenden, has a section " Of the Nature of Claikgeis." He tells various stories as to the proof of their existence. " All trees that are cassin in the seis, be process of tyme, apperis first wormeetin, and

in the small boris and hollis thairof growis small wormis.
First they schaw their heid and feit, and last of all they
schaw their plumis and wyngis. Finaly, quhen thay ar
cumyn to the just measure and quantite of geis, thay fle
in the air, as other fowlis dois." He adds the story of a
tree cast ashore in Aberdeenshire, near Pitsligo Castle,
which was full of these " claiks." Similar examples had
been observed at Dundee and Leith, and the particular information of Master Alexander Galloway, parson of Kinkell,
in Aberdeenshire, who, in a tangle of seaweed, apparently
full of mussel-shells, opened one of them, " he saw na fische
in it, bot ane perfit schapin foule, smal and gret, ay effering
to the quantite of the schell." The tradition and belief
was almost universal throughout Europe, and is referred
to in the proceedings of the Lateran Council, 1215, when
the eating of these " claikis " was forbidden during Lent.
John Gerarde, of London, Master in Chirurgie, who published an " Herball " in 1597, gives in it a picture of the
tree, with birds issuing from its branches and swimming
away into the sea. He states that these trees grow in the
" Islands called Orchades," and from them " those little
living foulis, whom we call Barnakles." He had seen
specimens. There are also later accounts ; that of Johnston
will be presently referred to.

Sir Robert Moray, one of " His Majestie's Council for
the Kingdom of Scotland," relates that in " the Island of
East [Uist ?] " he saw " a cut of a large Firr tree " on which
" there still hung multitudes of little shells, having within
them little Birds, perfectly shaped, supposed to be Barnacles.
. . This Bird, in every Shell that I opened, as well as the
least as the biggest, I found so curiously and completely
formed, that there appeared nothing wanting, as to the
internal parts, for making up a perfect sea-fowl." They
had little bills " like that of goose, the Eyes marked, the
Head, Neck, Wings, Tail, and Feet formed, the Feathers
every where perfectly shap'd, and blackish coloured ; and
the Feet like those of other Waterfowl, to my best

remembrance ; all being Dead and Dry."[1] The picture from Gerarde's " Herball " is given by Muller. Another old illustration and description is given in the " Museum Wormianum," where the same story is related, an account being added of those found near Dumbarton Castle. The author states that, as to the generation of these birds, authors differ. The passage is worth reading.[2]

Maier tells us in his preface to the reader that, when doubtful of the fact, he had corroborative information from a *doctor of Scotland*. It may be interesting to ascertain who this was. A famous Scotchman, Duncan Liddel, is found at Rostock in the early part of this century. He was a native of Aberdeen, and a graduate at King's College, the University of Boece ; went abroad, like so many other enterprising Scotsmen of the period, to study at the continental seats of learning. He became a teacher of mathematics and philosophy at Frankfort. " He next removed to *Rostock*, in North Germany, and finally settled at Helmsted, in Brunswick. He became rector of the University there, composing and publishing several works, which spread his name and fame over Europe.[3] Another scholar who travelled much abroad, and who was of Scotch origin, was Doctor John Johnston, who studied in Prussia, at St Andrews, at Cambridge, and at Leyden, where he eventually settled. He was a correspondent of Cambden. In his " Thaumatographia Naturalis," Amsterdam, 1632, which is dedicated to the famous John Valentine Andreas, whom Johnston calls his special friend, we have (p. 240) an account of the Barnacle—" Scoti nomine clackgeese dignantor." He describes it as black on the breast, otherwise of a gray colour, being bred out of the decay and putrescence of wood, but when it falls into water, revives and becomes a living bird, " cresit illa in Insula Pomonia in Scotia versus aquilonem." He quotes Boece at great length, Isidore, Olaus Magnus, Alexander ab Alexandro, Gesner.

---

[1] Max Muller, " Lectures on Science of Language," ii. 585, *et seq.*
[2] " Museum Wormianum," by Olaus Worm, Amsterdam, Elzevier, 1655, p. 257. [3] " Pro. Soc. Antiq. Scot.," xi. 451-2.

As an appendix to one of his chapters, he quotes from Maier's treatise. He designates our author as "medicus nobilissimus."

It appears that Joseph Scaliger agreed with the opinion of Johnston that the "claikgeese" were bred "ex putredine vestustorum Navigiorum," adding that as no trees grew in the extreme North of Scotland, the birds could not hang from their branches.[1]

Wallace, the first historian of Orkney, makes small account of our "claikes." He says—"Sometimes are cast in by the sea, pieces of Trees, and sometimes Hogsheads of Wine and Brandie, all covered over with an innumerable plenty of these Creatures which they call Cleek-goose, though I take them to be nothing else but a kind of sea-shell (the *Concha anatifera*), which you may see by its Figure." The figured shell is exactly of the shape given by Gerarde and Worm. Wallace also gives us a picture of the goose itself. [2]

Mackaile, an apothecary at Aberdeen, and who about the Restoration period practised medicine in Kirkwall, expressed his unbelief "that these geese are generate out of trees. For I have not only seen an old tree full of these shells like to muscles, wherein they are said to be found, but also fresh stern posts of ships which no man would believe to be six months wrought." [3]

Having thus given an account from different authors of the "Tree-bird," I shall proceed to lay before the reader abstracts of Maier's volume.

The manner of the reproduction of creatures and vegetables varies. Some act by friction, others expel the seed into the waters. Vegetables, metals—all have a peculiar method of generation, and some take a very long time to arrive at any perfection. Many animalculæ are bred from putrid matter by the heat of the sun. Is it wonderful, therefore, that life should be continued without

[1] Irving, "Scottish Writers," i. 7.   [2] "Descrip. of Orkney," 1693, 17-18.
[3] Quoted by Barry, "Hist. of Orkney," 450-1.

those we regard as parents ? No, for God has created all things varied and wonderful. Even in the vilest material great mysteries may be discovered. Diodorus Siculus tells us that mice, and even serpents, are generated in Egypt, with many other creatures, from the mud of the Nile. Hornets are produced out of the putrid flesh of horses ; and do not fruits, apples, plums, cherries, pears, produce worms ? Vermin are bred in dogs' tongues ; worms are grown in the heart of roses ; and even in man himself, in putrid ulcers, living creatures are bred. The matrix wherein these are generated is that part of the animal or vegetable where the heat, working on the viscid material, disposes to putrefaction. So surely it may be believed that these birds in the Orkneys are produced not from the ordinary seed, nor from an egg, but by an admirable manner in the very innermost theatre of Nature herself.

The author relates the story of the Tree-bird from various authors. Oaks and trees produce flies and moths, others produce worms. In some countries trees attract water to such an extent that they supply drink to men and flocks. So, too, in Egypt, where there is no rain, the Nile, by its annual inundation, fills the surrounding regions with riches. So why should not the Orkneys, and other isles of that far northern region, produce these birds ? But authors of long ago have made mention of them—Cardan, Du Bertas, Munsterus, Gyraldus who finds them in Ireland, and specially Hector Boethius. Does not Plutarch ask the question, Was the egg existing before the fowl ? He then relates at length the story as told by Boethius, and makes some reference to strange growths in the dykes bounding North Holland. It is not to be supposed, however, that the ocean, or the fecundity of the waters, are the causes of the generation of the Tree-birds.

Still, consider the wonderful fecundity of the sea, which produces such a multitude of fish, even whales sixty feet long, thirty feet across, which Pliny tells are found in the gulfs of Arabia. One author has enumerated 176 different kinds of fish. Look, too, at the beauty of the shells. In the year 1611, when at Rotterdam, Peter Carpenter showed me nearly one thousand different forms of these. Here, surely, we have a proof of the luxuriancy of Nature. Recall again the old stories of Neptune and of the sea-born Nymphs.

The Tree-birds are doubtless born of the heat distributed in the putrid material, for without heat no generation can take place. Flies, frogs, and the like, are produced from water, earth, and heat. Yes! the Sun is the father—the oil, pitch, resin in the trees, are the rudimentary matters on which the Sun acts.

But it may be asked, Why are these creatures produced in this particular form? Just as in a piece of amber forms are sometimes enclosed, so here the form of birds is produced—suitable to the material—as bees from worms. These birds, it is true, do not breed between themselves, neither do mules. They are so made to show the power and the variety of Nature, and how nature is rich beyond imagination in expedient, and full of curious art and power in production.

And the proper end of the generation of this bird exhibits from its double nature, vegetable and animal, a type of Christ, God, and man.

The author relates the beautiful old story of Alcyone, who, marrying Ceyx by presumption, was overwhelmed by grief. Ceyx perished in a shipwreck, and Alcyone threw herself into the sea; but, by the pity of the gods, the pair were changed into birds. It was believed that during the seven days before and the seven days after the shortest day of the year, while these birds were breeding, the sea remained calm.

> " Alcyone compressed,
> Seven days sits brooding on her floating nest ;
> A wintry queen ! her sire at length is kind,
> Calms every storm and hu-hes every wind ;
> Prepares his empire for his daughter's ease,
> And for his hatching nephews smoothes the seas."

Maier again enters upon his mystical story. Alcyone typifies the Church, which, tossed on the waves of the world, experiences the rage of tyrants. But the Orkney bird has a higher meaning. It is Christ, who, without father or ordinary mother, was born. It is thus that the Son of God was born without human father and of a Virgin, who was such before and after his birth. But the world will not tolerate mysteries. The tree from which he hangs is the cross, and by it is man elevated to heaven. He bare the cross and our sins on His shoulders, to cast our sins into the bottomless ocean ; and by virtue of this tree and its fruit were God and man conciliated. O ! the goodness of God and the vastness of His mercy to man, who, without this Remedy, would have perished ; so awful was the first fall of man, that without the death of all in One could not man be restored. Thus, by the unerring wisdom of God, our very nature has been carried beyond the stars. What a splendour does that Ruby and that Carbuncle display ! Thus does this poor Tree-bird display the Divine Idea, and furnishes from that Remote Spot a hieroglyphic, not merely of the Church, in the Alcyonic story, but the grand story of the God man, the Mediator Christ, who may be known not merely by the miracle in Nature, but by the divine history and the highest flights of philosophy.

The seventh chapter of Maier's work treats of the Tartarian Lamb—a vegetable-animal or zoophite. The world is God's book, and all its volumes are open to teach us the wonders of His hand.

Sigismund, Baron de Herbestein, the author of the " Little Theatre of the World," tell us that, near the Caspian Sea and the River Volga, in a country inhabited by Tartars, flourishes what the natives call Bonaretz—that means a little lamb. It is shaped like that animal, having footstalks instead of legs, and is said to eat up the grass and herbs round about it, after which it dies. Its skin is exactly like wool, short and curly, and being dressed by tanners, can be used instead of fur to line garments. No beast of prey will eat it except the wolf. The wool is so exactly like that of a young lamb, that a difference can scarcely be detected It is even believed that when cut up blood streams forth, and its internal parts are found just like those of an animal. It is indeed a hieroglyphic of that Lamb which takes away the sin of the world; all in Nature is double, spiritual things being seen by natural things.[1] A learned naturalist, Dr Kempfer, is, however, of opinion that the story of the Lamb and its fine fur took rise from the custom that the Tartars and Persians have of " ripping up the Dam and taking out the Fœtus only for the sake·of the fur," then of so " delicate a grain that after cutting off the extremities it scarce resembles a lamb skin, and might easily deceive the ignorant, who would be apt to take it for the downy skin of a gourd."

We next have an account of the Dragon's Blood tree, a vegetable of India. Doctors differ in regard to this sanguine substance, the origin of which was long disputed, some believing it was the real blood either of a dragon or an elephant. Monardus, bishop of Cartagena, however, discovered the tree from which this blood is produced, which is the gum of the tree. The true explanation is that " the gum we corruptly call gumdragon issues spontaneously from this plant toward the end of June and the two following months, at which time the nutricious juice, thickened by the heat, bursts the vessels that contain it, and being coagulated into small threads, these make their way, by little and little, through the bark, are hardened in the air, and formed either into lumps or slender pieces twisted like worms."[2]

We have also the passion flower or plant, formed like a rose, in which are found all the various figures of the passion of Christ.

In Egypt we are told that eggs are hatched by artificial means. Truly, there is nothing new under the sun, not even

---

[1] See also " Wonders of Nature and Art," Lon. 1768, iii. 74,
[2] " Wonders of Nature and Art," iii, 241.

incubation. The story is to be seen in Diodorus Siculus. The custom still prevails, and thousands of fowls are thus produced. It is merely a chemical process and easily understood. Other tales are added in regard to the production of silk-worms, ants, and other creatures—full, indeed, of marvels. He returns to his theory of the production of verminous life through putrescence—that scorpions are born from herbs, and that from human corpses, worms and serpents are bred, serpents in which devils live, full of venom. This is supported by a story told by St Augustine in one of his sermons, that when certain sepulchres or graves were opened, toads were found in the brain pan, serpents were crawling about the loins, and worms in the interior parts of the body. Behold, cries St Augustine, what we are and into what we shall devolve. Even from kings are produced fleas and bugs. What do these facts teach us ? That man within himself and without is but the habitation and the food of worms, and thus does the glory of the world perish.

In England are many strange creatures to be found. Two dogs that lived in a cave were shewn to be demons. There, too, are found, as related by Henry, Bishop of Winchester, toads with golden chains round their necks, and from solid rocks, toads, living and moving, have been taken. Maier enters into a long discussion as to how toads can exist in rocks, hermetically sealed up, without food. He seems to think it must be the heat which preserves them. We hear next the story of Typhon and the tale of Osiris; already in the "Aurea Mensa" and in "Atalanta" has been given the real explanation of these hieroglyphics. They relate solely to chemical matters, and to these treatises the reader is referred.

The story of Phœnix is next discussed. The ancient and vulgar opinions in regard to this fire-bird are quite erroneous. It was understood by the most ingenious Egyptians and Greeks really to refer to a chemical process, to chemistry, the mother of the arts. The labours of Hercules, the mistakes of Ulysses, the dangers undergone

by Jason, the flight of Atalanta, the Golden Fleece, the
Trojan expedition, and also the story of the Phœnix, with
innumerable other such-like tales, we have thus expounded.
The story of the Phœnix is not unlike that of the Orkney
bird, being produced by the sun through heat.

> " His nest on oaken boughs begins to build,
> Or trembling tops of palms ; and first he draws
> The plan with his broad bill and crooked claws,
> Nature's artificers, and rises round them with the spoil
> Of Cassia, Cinnamon, and stems of Nard
> (For softness strew'd beneath) his funeral bed is reared ;
> Funeral and bridal both, and all around
> The borders with corruptless myrrh are crown'd,
> On this incumbent, till ethereal flame
> First catches, then consumes the costly frame ;
> Consumes him too, as on the pile he lies.
> He lived on odours, and in odours dies.
> An infant Phœnix from the former springs,
> His father's heir, and from his tender wings
> Shakes off the parent dust." [1]

Then what absurd and puerile tales do even the most
learned and wise amongst the old pagans relate as to the
origin of the first men. Some believed that at first mankind were of both sexes in one ; others that man sprang
from the earth ; others that man sprang from the gods ;
others that men were originally of gigantic stature, that
they sprang from stones. There is no doubt that giants
existed such as are described as Titans and killed by
lightning, but this is a chemical mystery, as are the stories
of Typhon, Briareus, Polyphemus, Anteus, Atlas, Gyges,
and a multitude more. In Crete, by an earthquake, a
body, forty-six cubits long, was disclosed. Ancient authors
give many other instances, as in Berosus and Saxo Grammaticus. Then we have the story of Goliath the Philistine.

In England, in the reign of King Stephen, near a certain
village called Wulspittle, were found two children, a boy
and a girl, whose whole bodies were of a green colour.
These children were brought to holy baptism, but the boy
died a short time thereafter. But the girl lived.

---

[1] Ovid, " Metam.," xv.

The story of Tages, who first taught magic to the Romans and " acts prophetic," is given from Ovid :—

> " The swains who Tyrrhene furrows till'd
> When heaving up, a clod was seen to roll,
> Untouch'd, self-mov'd, and big with human soul.
> The spreading mass in former shape depos'd
> Began to shoot, and arms and legs disclos'd,
> Till form'd a perfect man, the living mold
> Op'd its new mouth, and future truths foretold ;
> And Tages, nam'd by natives of the place,
> Taught arts prophetic to the Tuscan race."

Other strange births are in the thirteenth chapter recalled—Pallas, Hebe, Bacchus—

> " Jove took him from the blasted womb,
> And, if on ancient tales we may rely,
> Inclos'd the abortive infant in his thigh.
> Here, when the babe had all his time fulfilled,
> Juno first took him for her foster child.
> Then the Niseans, in their dark abode,
> Nurs'd secretly with milk the thriving god."

The relations between the human fœtus and the philosophical and chemical fœtus are full of analogies. The stories of Helen, of Castor, of Clytemnestra, of Læda, all have philosophic meanings hidden under their histories. Then, lastly, there is the mandrake, a very wonderful thing (if it is true), like an infant, living, but black, which crieth sharp cries when pulled up out of the ground. All these have reference also to our sacred birth in baptism, through the application of the sacred chrism.

It is said that commerce between men and spirits produce Incubi et Succubi, and this is partly true and partly false. That men have been produced by the overshadowing of a phantasm is told of Plato and Merlin. Alexander the Great is said to have been persuaded that he was the son of Jupiter Ammon. Hercules is said to have been the son of Jove and Alcmena. Hercules' story is an allegory, and the story of Merlin is to be rejected altogether. But such stories are common enough, and to be found even amongst the Tartars. Is such a thing possible ?—I mean whether incubi and succubi have the

K

power of generation. It may be possible by demoniac power, and monsters may be so generated. Peter Loyerus, in his " Liber de Spectris," tells a strange story as to a girl called Philinion, who, to the inconsolable grief of her parents, having died, is washed, and her body purified by odours and aromatic balsams, is placed in the tomb, with her jewels and other ornaments. About six months after, a youth named Machatis came to visit her parents. He retires to rest in an upper chamber. In the night, he hears the voice of a girl saluting him, who. laughing, enters into conversation with him. She being extremely beautiful, he desires her greatly, and lies down with her. Charito, the girl's mother, having heard her, came running, and cries that it is the voice of her daughter, who had been dead six months before. Eventually is was proved to be a phantasm, and poor Machatis paid dearly, by an early death, for his friendship with that " cadaver." [1]

We are next introduced to the subject of Lycanthropes, or Wolfmen. These are referred to more than once by Heroditus, as found amongst the Scythians ; and are the result of the connection of men with demons. Olaus Magnus also has some curious stories in regard to them. They do much evil, they tear children to pieces, they slaughter flocks, they destroy food, and do all kinds of mischief. These creatures can remain in this state for twelve days, when again gathering themselves together at a certain river, crossing it, become as men and return home. One, being caught, was brought in chains before Garzonious, a great Russian chief, who asked him if it were true that he could transform himself into a wolf, declared it to be most true. He was asked to do so. Retiring apart, and by some diabolic mystery, he returned with flaming eyes, a horrible appearance, but two dogs having been let loose upon him, he reassumed his human form. Instances are given—one related to Maier by a friend.

[1] As to this curious subject, see H. Jennings' " Rosicrucians," third edition, p. 401, *et seq.*

Other animal forms are said to be assumed by human beings, cases of which are related by Saxo Grammaticus and St Augustine. But the saint, though relating the story, evidently did not believe it. He merely mentions it as a strange tale " of the Arcadians, who, swimming over a certain lake, became wolves, and lived with the wolves of the ¦woods ; and if they eate no man's flesh, at nine year's end, swimming over the said lake, they became men again." [1]

The last chapter is " De Geniis," of different sorts— " Sylvani, Lamiæ "—satyrs and witches.

Maier commences with a commentary on the passage in Genesis relating the connection of the sons of God with the daughters of men, and holds that it refers to the connections of the children of Seth and those of Cain, and has not any demoniac meaning. The ancient genii, who appear in Roman history, were of a divine nature—the gods local of places, or of things, or of special men. Lemures, hares, nocturnal earthly creatures, and phantasms. These could be evolved by magical art. Stories are quoted from Jamblicus, and of Apollonius of Tyana, and of the horrors and impurities of witches. Lamiæ—spectres in the form of lovely girls, beautifully dressed, and full of " sweet cunning." The old story of Lilith is not forgotten. These evil spirits have power to persuade mankind to deeds of impurity. At night they lie down beside youths, and, exciting their " natural force," cause pollutions. They can even assume the form of women, and their general conduct is not merely impudent but lascivious and contrary to nature, and indeed a veil had better be drawn over their ultimate intentions and actions.

Then follows the " Conclusio Tractatus." The writer claims to have shown that what seems contrary to nature is really wrought by the omnipotent power of God, and part of His divine plan.

[1] "De Civit. Dei.," xviii. 17.   See also Scott's "Letters on Demonology," &c., 211.

SEPTIMANA PHILOSOPHICA. Qua Ænigmata Aureola de omni Naturæ genere a Salomone Israelitarum Sapientissimo Rege, et Arabiæ Regina Saba, nec non Hyramo, Tyri Principe, sibi invicem in modum Colloquii proponuntur et enodantur. Ubi passim novæ, at veræ, cum ratione et experientia convenientes, rerum naturalium causæ exponuntur et demonstrantur, figuris cupro incisis singulis diebus adjectis, Authore Michaele Maiero, Imperialis Consistorii Comite, Eq. Ex. Med. D. et Cæs. Majest. olim Aulico, nunc illustriss Principis ac Dn. Mauritii, Hassiæ Landgravii, &c., Archiatro. Francofurti Typis Hartmanni Palthenii. Sumptibus Lucæ Iennis, 1620.

4to. Title surrounded with pictured scenes, the upper part representing the conference of the two Kings and the Queen of Sheba, with secretaries and people in a large hall. At the inner side, four medallions ; upper two of the earth in different states of development ; scene, miners and smiths, a female praying ; below, at the inner side, "Timor Dni est initium Sapientiæ, Syr. I." On the outer side, at the bottom, "Eloquentia Dei donum et opus est. Exod. 4 " ; a woman with a wreathed caduceus, then Adam and Eve below the tree ; higher up, scene probably referring to the naming of the animals ; at the upper part a scene, probably Garden of Eden. Follows " Oda alcaica," by John Flitner. Then the dedication, 4pp., to Christian Wilhelm, Archbishop of Magdeburg, Primate of Germany, " Domino suo clementissimo." Maier addresses him as most reverend archbishop, illustrious prince, most clement lord. He prays that the one true God, omnipotent and merciful, who so well knows our needs and our weaknesses, may bless this endeavour. He refers to the dignity of the physician and the chemist, and to the fact that Solomon, the most wise of men, must have had some knowledge of the Hermetic art. He asks him to accept the dedication, and commends him to God's constant care. Dated at Magdeburg, 11th Jan. 1620. The preface to the reader and an epigrammic poem by the author, 3pp. ; then the author's portrait, followed by a poetical piece by Daniel Rabtrecht of Brandeburg, 2 pp. ; then an alcaic ode by Jacob Pontanus, 3 pp. ; an epigram, "in effigiem authoris," by John Flitner, 1p. ; index ænigmatum, 14 pp. ; 1 page errata ; the work itself, 228 pp. ; index rerum et verborum, 52 pp. ; 1 folding plate, and plates in the text.

—AUTHOR'S LIBRARY.

A chapter for each day. The work begins with an account of the persons and circumstances at the meeting of Solomon, the Queen of Sheba, and Hiram, Prince of Tyre. After a discussion in regard to the country and antecedents of the Queen, the narrative proceeds to relate their meeting at Jerusalem, in the palace of Solomon, who, having greeted his friends, addressed them in a speech. He sets apart a week (six days) for a philosophic discussion or instruction, commencing with the subject " de Cælo et Elementis." The Queen of Sheba asks the first question, " Tell us, therefore, most sapient King, which is the greatest and most important part in occult philosophy, that concerning the Heaven or the Earth ? " Solomon answers that earth, being the centre, and the heavens merely the circumference, the earth fixed and stable, the heavens merely air and changeable, the earth is the noblest part. The earth is regarded as the centre of the world. The sun is the heart of the heavens, and from it flows forth light, heat, and power. A folding plate shows the idea of the Universe—the earth, " centrum mundi," with the motions of the sun and moon. The " Primum Mobile " surrounds the whole. The Queen demands by what chain the heaven and earth are joined together. Solomon answers the same that joins the tree and the apple, the mother and the fœtus. Which, then, existed first, the heavens or the earth ? Solomon refers to the old question, Did the hen or the egg first exist ? A " responsio circularis " is given. The earth could not exist without the heavens, nor the heavens without the earth. The questions continue, Hiram intervening at times with notes of praise of Solomon's wisdom, and his own desire of certain information.

To the eighteenth "Ænigma"—Is the heavens masculine or is the earth?"—the answer is given, the earth. Hiram seems particularly interested in the conjunction of Sol and Luna, particularly in what place that event took place. The day now nearing its close, Solomon turns to the Queen of Sheba and puts certain astronomical questions, particularly as to the position of the sun to, and its distance from, the earth. Hiram is then questioned in regard to the moon. On page 31 a full-sized picture is given of Sol acting on Luna, and producing Europa. The chapter closes with an inquiry directed by Hiram to Solomon in regard to the cause of the lunar light and eclipses.

The second day treats " de Meteoris seu imperfecte mixtis "—showers, dew, snow, hail, origin of springs, comets, thunderbolts, lightnings, clouds, thunder, wind, rainbows. The discussion begins by the Queen of Sheba in a question as to condensation and rarification. Questions follow as to the colours of the clouds, their resolution into water, the operation of dews and showers, the cause of vapours. At Ænigma 56, Hiram again, at the request of Solomon, intervenes as to the origin and uses of winds, and then addresses questions to Solomon as to hail, frost, snow, and ice. A diagram is given explaining the cause of these by the remoteness of the sun, and the consequent obliquity of its rays. The cause of lightning, its power, its deadly result— a similar power of quick penetration is contained in, and seen by the use of the Philosopher's Stone, which is by Lullius and others likened to the operation of lightning on metallic substances. The cause of the rainbow is demonstrated in two cuts. The cause of comets, astrological nativities, and other astronomical questions are then referred to.

The conference of the third day, " de Terræ fossilibus," is opened by an ovation from Solomon, who, after quoting the story of Thales having been the first to predict an eclipse of the sun, goes on to detail the opinions of Plato, Cicero, and others, as to the fires in the centre of the earth. That there is the alembic of Nature, a catalogue is given of the results in precious stones, medicines, and divers products. The Queen of Sheba then enters on the story of Cadmus and the dragon, Typhon and Echidna, and goes on to question Solomon as to " Sal, Sulphur, et Mercurium," and to inquire whence " argentum vivum," which is the material of the work, is to be had. The Queen seems to be equally well-informed as to the philosophic tincture, the Stone, and other like items, with Solomon. She tells him that the Stone is Apis, that is Osiris. Solomon goes on and demands, " Quis est pater lapidis, et quis avus ? " The Queen answers that Saturn is grandfather, Chiron tutor, Vulcan præceptor, and Jupiter the father.

The fourth day's conference refers to vegetable life. A very pretty cut heads the chapter, in which trees, wheat, and a laid-out garden are shown.

Solomon begins with his usual ovation. The fourth page of the book of the great world is now unfolded. Whence did Antony the Eremite gain his great knowledge ? He had no written book or great library. It was in the contemplation of the world, in Nature, that he found that knowledge. So now we open the great " herbarium." There are two different sorts of vegetables—those grown in the ordinary processes of Nature from seed of the same species, and those produced by the putrefaction of matter. Earth and water are really the parents of vegetables. Air is resolved into water, and so is the food of plants. A garden is both pleasant and useful. Epicurus was the first who within the walls of Athens laid out a garden. He lived in it, and taught in it.

THE ROSE.

The first of all flowers. The most lovely and perfect, sweet, like a virgin ; guarded, its sweetness defended by

thorns. Has it not a place among Philosophers ? Solomon
answers the Queen that Philosophers have built many
Rosaries, in which have grown different rose-plants, greater
and less, bearing both red and white roses. For divers
reasons are the natural roses the emblems of philosophic
substance. Red and white, the emblems of Gold and
Silver. The centre of the rose is green—an emblem of
the green Lion which philosophers know well. The Rose
is a pleasure to the senses and life of man, on account of its
sweet odour, its beauty and salubrity. So is the philosophic rose—exhilarating, helpful, refreshing the heart,
strengthening the brain. As the rose turns to the sun,
and is refreshed by the rain, so is the philosophic matter
prepared in blood, grown in light, and so made perfect.
Vulcan gives his heat, Juno his shower, which is announced
by the rainbow. Why, then, are roses both white and red ?
The colours proceed from the qualities of the elements.
The red side of the apple is that which lies to the sun's
influence. The colour of the rose all red proceeds from its
ephemeral nature, the white from the sulphur in the elements producing the flowers—the lily, hyacinth, narcissus,
the crocus, and the herb moly. A number of questions are
solved in regard to the nature, growth, and properties of
wheat. The invention of wine, not by Bacchus, but by
Noah. Questions also follow as to the wood in which
Hercules killed the Nemean lion, and the gardens of the
Hesperides. These are given an alchemic meaning, and
then are followed by a number of occult solutions of the
nature of other trees and plants—for instance, " smilax
vero virgo alba, et crocus juvenis rubeus."

The fifth day's discussion is "de animalibus." The plate
shows them on the land and in the sea, frisking and dis-
porting themselves ; in the air birds flying, and on the top
of a hill the far-famed phœnix in a flaming nest. The
land animals are recognisable, but the sea creatures are
both fierce and grotesque. Their differing natures were

well known to Adam. They were given by the Creator to
minister to mankind. A new nature became theirs through
the fall ; yet, having more sense than even the Spartans,
they neither gave way to inebriety nor vice. The Queen
of Sheba asks the reason why the ancient Egyptians held
the bull or ox in such estimation. Solomon answers with
a description of Apis which was an ox—black—with a
white spot on the forehead. The soul of Osiris animated
this chosen animal. Osiris is the sun, and the white spot
represents the moon. The camel is an emblem of Saturn.
The story of the Trojan horse is well known to philosophers—designed by Pallas, it has an arcane signification.
The lion is known in philosophy as of different colours—
green, white, red, tawny—with wings and without. Atalanta and Hippomenes are figured by red lions, the female
fleeing and the masculine pursuing, throwing the golden
apples, are at last " vase, coeuntes in rubeam tincturam
vertuntur." The allegorical connection of bear, wolf, dog,
ram, panther, leopard, lynx, follow. The Queen asks why
do the Egyptians honour the cat ? Its eyes change with
the increase or decrease of the moon, and at night the cat
sees best. The Cynocephalus—Anubis—bears the same
relation to the sun that the cat does to the moon.

Birds then come under review. Those having relation
to occult philosophy are the hen, the raven, the pigeon, the
peacock, the vulture, the eagle, the ibis, and the phœnix.
The raven, in its colour, prefigures the beginning of " the
work "; the peacock the changing colours in the operation.
The allegory of the phœnix is referred to at much greater
length. It denotes the philosophic tincture. It is of the
size of the eagle with a golden band around its neck. It
lives 660 years, and expires amid the odours of incense ; is
sacred to the sun.

The references to fishes come next. The story of the
Murex—first white, then red. The story of the fish Oxy-
ringus, which possesses shining eyes and white colour, but
has a green back, black and white feathers, with a long

green tail. This is the fish which swallowed the " pudenda
Osiris " in " Nilum abjecta." The distress caused to Isis by
the loss of these was the reason of the worship of Priapus.
Isis caused a golden phallus to be made, and solemn rites of
worship in connection with it to be instituted. These spread
over Greece, Asia, and Europe, among the Hebrews, " Voca-
verunt Phegor vel Beelphægor." It refers to the philosophic
sulphur, combustible and burning. The conversation on
this part of the subject is very properly restricted to Hiram
and Solomon. The Queen, however, reappears at " Ænigma
261 "—anent the Crocodile. From an egg it grows to the
length of twenty-two cubits. It lies on dry land during
the day, but spends the night in the river Nile. Cities
have been built in its honour. It has very strong teeth
and an impenetrable hide. It also refers to the sulphur
found in our philosophic Nile The Queen then asks information in regard to the two serpents twisted around the
Caduceus of Mercury and of Esculapius. They refer to the
double nature of Mercury—the sun hot, the moon cold,
together the nature of Mercury. One is feminine, the other
masculine. The Salamander, the Basilisk, and the Silk-
worm have their mystic meanings.

The last day's conference is " de homine." The cut
represents a globe in a frame, supported on the one side by
a masculine figure with a compass, on the other by a
skeleton, the latter holding a vase with smoking contents.
Man is a mixture of audacity and prudence. He is the
" Parvus Mundus "—the little world—Microcosmos. Of
this lesser world Europe is the head, Africa the breast, there
is the heart—Sol. Africa is the hottest part. So in the
breast is the vital heat of man. The similitude of the heart
and the sun is drawn out at some length. In the breast
the diaphram explicits earth, the lungs air, the heart fire,
the blood water. The Nile represents the blood flowing to
and from the heart—" nix et aqua Nile "—in epistola
Rhasis. Asia is the name of the lower parts—the belly,

&c. Here in the stomach is prepared the nutrition necessary to the body, with the excreta, the seminal juices. So Asia is the most fertile of all parts, produces more fruits and animals, metals, and aromatics than the other parts. As man took his rise and as his regeneration was wrought out in Asia, as there lay Paradise, where it was said to man " increase and multiply," so may the allegory be read of the lower parts of man. The Queen adds that philosophers say there are three stones—vegetable, animal, and mineral— that are in virtues diverse. Why, asks Solomon of the Queen, is the stone called animal ? Sol—" animal magnum," " et Sal Ammoniacus sit ex eo." So is Luna a plant, " et Sal Alcali sit ex eo." Mercury is called a stone mineral, " et sit Sal commune de eo."

With "Ænigma 319," Solomon concludes the explanation of the Microcosmos, adding that their labours being now over, according to divine precepts they shall rest to-morrow, being the Sabbath day, in which all—angels, men, the world itself—shall see an image of the rest and joy of eternity. " Deo sit gloria pro hactenus sua concessa nobis gratia. Finis."

A full and excellent index completes the " Septimana Philosophica."

CIVITAS CORPORIS hnmani, a tyrannide Arthritica vindicata. Hoc est, Podagræ, Chiragræ, et Gonagræ, quæ, velut tyranni immanissimi artus extremos obsident, et excruciant, Methodica Curatio. Duobus auxiliis potissimum instituta, ac deinde latius clarissimorum, præsentim Germaniæ, Medicorum testimoniis comprobata, inque Medicina Candidatorum gratiam atque utilitatem concinnata et edita; Authore Michaele Maiero, Com. Pal. Phil. et Med. D. Equite nob. exempto, olim Cæs. Maiest. Rudolphi II., aulico Medico, &c. Francofurti, Impensis Lucæ Jennis. Anno [M]DCXXI.

8vo ; 216 pp. ; one cut, p. 167. "Ex dono Alexr. Reid, Med. Doct"—a great benefactor to the University of Aberdeen. (See Records Marischal College. i. 226, et seq.)
—UNIVERSITY OF ABERDEEN.

This work commences with a dedication to medical men and medical students, and to all afflicted with gout. A warning is given against the nostrums of empirics, and the author's method explained. This dedication is dated at Magdeburg in the month of August 1620. Two pages, containing an epigram, follow. Then a preface addressed to the reader, containing the division into heads of the Tractate. There are twelve chapters.

In the first chapter the "Civitas Corporis humani" is declared to be the lesser world. As the greater world of the universe consists of different members—sun, moon, planets, angels, and other creatures—so the lesser "civitas"

consists of different parts and members. The "cives" are
the parts differentiated by the anatomical art with their
wonderful functions, which should, in all their perfection,
be offered as a sacrifice and a Hetacomb to God. It is true,
indeed, that not in this present state and world can the
full knowledge of God be obtained. Even the sacred
Revelation does not disclose a thousandth part of His
glory. How then can a man of three or four cubits in
height extend to the infinitude of omnipotency? But as
we know the sun by its brightness, some can sufficiently
know God even for eternal life by the word of His revelation. It is our duty then, as guardians of the "civitas"
of the human body, to observe the different citizens, or
members, their names, order, places, functions, and offices
politic. As in music there are different tones, all fitting
into one perfect harmony, so in the body the different
members are united in one society. These are distinguished
by different names, orders, and places. From the belly and
the organs of generation we rise to higher things—to the
Head, the seat or arx of the intellect. Now, as civil states
have magistracy and offices which are duly elected, and all
should be united in obedience to God, so is it in the bodily
"civitas." The heart is the first magistrate or ruler. From
it do the other members receive their power and order. It
is placed in the centre. Under it do the five senses act,
and through its power is the office of generation accomplished.

The second chapter begins by declaring that in the body
politic there are three States. First, the King or Prince;
second, the order of Aristocracy; and thirdly, the Demo-
cracy. Undoubtedly the monarchical form of government
is the most perfect. What form of government then exists
in the human centres? It is not exactly regal, but may
rather be compared to the order of the Venetian Republic,
in which a number of magnates reign under a prince of
limited power. The heart is that prince. Under it the
throat, liver, œsophagus, the teeth, the tongue, and the

other members of this aristocracy perform their functions.
It is in the inferior parts of the body furthest from the
heart that the tyranny of the enemies of the " civitas " is
to be found, and then the hands and feet suffer from gout
and the like diseases. The deficiences in work and diligence of the liver, the stomach, and other parts cause the
defect.

The next chapter treats of the remedies in general to be
used in regard to defects in the oligarchy of the " civitas."
All must do their parts properly and equally, else, like a
sedition in the State politic, relapses and troubles will
arise. So is it in this other " civitas." The cloaca must
be free and unimpeded; the house must be free from
noxious matters. Gluttony, lust, drunkenness, and the like
must first of all be banished. This will be of the greatest
service to the medical man. The mind must be freed from
evil and be purged from vice. In this the medical man
himself must give an example. Temperance and a continent life are the powers which will put in right motion
the army of the " civitas." Gout is ever the companion of
riches and delicate living. Such persons give the armies of
the " civitas " too much to do—then they rebel. Venus
and Bacchus are the greatest friends of gout. Hippocrates
has laid down a golden rule:—Be continent, be active in
labour, and abstain from supper once a week. Venery
debilitates the body and weakens its action, rendering the
blood thin and cold. Wine, again, causes crudity and
weakness of the nerves. Then is born the natural daughter
of both—gout.

The next chapter—the fourth—treats of the method of
cure and the specific remedies to be used. Those are treated
of under three heads. First, of the symptoms and indica-
tions of the disease. It is a mistake to think that regular
purgation debilitates the body ; on the contrary, it comforts
it. This being done, in the second place, a dose of " our
golden powder," to cause vomiting is to be administered ;
" evacuation by the mouth " being accomplished, a mer-

curial dose may be given. The stomach being thus free for its action, a cautious administration of food may then be received and sleep obtained. The second part of the cure consists of outward application to the affected parts of astringent and emollient applications—chamomile, thyme, wild marjoram being boiled together and applied on a poultice. Mineral applications are referred to, but not so strongly recommended as the vegetable decoctions. Objections to this treatment are heard and answered.

In the fifth chapter reference is made to the opinion of other medical authorities—Crato, Solenander, &c. These show the same opinion in regard to the diagnosis of the disease, and how the " civitas " is to be delivered from the attack of the tyrant. A number of others are quoted— Montanus, Leonus. They diagnose " origo fluxionis, et via." Leonus attributes the cause of the dieasse to the infrequent use of the bath and laxatives, to immoderate work, " lux venerea," much wine. Bacchus and Venus are at the bottom of the matter—" nam ut Venus enervat vires, sic copia vini." The nature of the " flux" is then discussed at considerable length. Rendeletius also shows the truth of the belief that from the parents the tendency to gout, &c., is derived. A number of prescriptions for pills are subsequently given—" hermodactyl," cinnamon, anise, aloes, red roses, mallows, " rhabarb," &c. Turpentine is also recommended, and prescriptions for a number of electuaries given. The head is to be washed with a special soapy ointment made of venice soap, ambergris, musk ; borage and syrup of poppies, with dates, are to be used in an emulsion.

The sixth chapter commences with the statement that as rivers flow from mountains and high lands into lower grounds, and at last into the sea, this motion has its counterparts in the lesser world of man, and this in *five* ways. Thus the steam from the extremities, from different parts of the body, must be allowed free egress. Maier takes an illustration from the overflow of rivers, that walls have to be built to keep the water from overflowing the land. The hands and feet are the banks of the leser world, and in them does the overflow or flux commonly appear. Guiacum, the well-known remedy, appears in a prescription of Donzellinus. The bandages are to be dipped in wine and salt.

In the seventh chapter the value of profuse perspiration is pointed out. It is thought that the disease descends in internal vapour to the head, and there condenses, and this not being worked off on account of want of exercise for the body, goes to the extremities, and forms the disease. Laziness is a predisposing cause.

As the drop falling again and again, not the strength, wears away the stone, so is it in the "civitas humani." The ant, continually at work, makes its home ; so the "gutta humoris" gradually forms the gouty secretion. As bad manners may be said to bring forward good and wholesome laws in the civil state, so is it in the human " civitas." By small and minute material, gradually accumulating, the outlet is choked and the disease begins, and then the need of special effort appears. For purgation, the use of asses' milk is advised ; but for stronger use, decoction of polypodium and anise for ten days, give a " happy " relief. There is also what is known as " the domestic syrup." It is of great use. Pages of other prescriptions follow.

The ninth chapter refers to the need of patience, and as to the treatment in the spasms and paroxysms of pain. How can these be avoided or shortened ? The spring and autumn are the more trying times. Purgatives are of great use, either by vomit or downwards. While these are being used, a decoction of acetic acid, myrtle berries, cypress, and acacia should be applied. There is also a powder to be applied, having been heated. It has a great many ingredients—lign-aloes, frankinsence, calamus, hyoschiamus, gum guiacum, &c., &c. Innumerable prescriptions and opinions of famous medical writers follow—one of which appears to be the laying of a puppy or young dog on the foot, the natural heat of which assists to dispel the trouble.

The tenth chapter refers to subsequent treatment of the distressed part. Fomentations are to be used made from herbs; also alum and sulphur, with a little frankincense and laurel berries. A vase made from oak only, of which a cut is given (p. 167), is of great use. It is double; the interior vase is that in which the hands or feet are to be placed and covered up. In the outer shell the decoction of herbs, &c., is to be placed. The heat apparently is to work on the distressed parts, which may be too tender to be put in the decoction itself.

In the eleventh chapter, sixteen " inimica" to recovery, and five " amica" are detailed. A story is told about the recovery of " Ponifesus Podager," who, by immersing his feet and legs, up to the knees, in wheat, had the trouble removed. Forty rules in life are given. Contentment with breakfast and supper is recommended. Sleep during the day is to be avoided, and eight hours sleep during the night is not to be exceeded. Rules for exercise follow. Quietness in life and freedom from perturbation of mind are of much value.

The last chapter contains some further advice and warnings—" et Deo optimo maximo hinc æternas laudes ac gratias referat, cui soli sit gloria. Finis."

The style of the treatise is lively and crisp, the matter interesting, full, and instructive ; the author's medical reading wide, and his quotations apt and proper.

L

MICHAELIS MAIERI CANTILENÆ INTELLECT-
UALES DE PHŒNICE REDIVIVO ; ou Chansons
Intellectuelles sur la Resurrection Du Phenix, Par
Michel Maier, &c. Traduites en François sur l'Original
Latin Par M. L. L. M. Le prix est de 3 livres relie.
A Paris, chez Debure l'aîne, Quai des Augustins,
à l'Image S. Paul. MDCCLVIII. Avec Approbation
Privilege du Roi.

aij-I ; 8vo ; 129 pp. ; avertissement, 5 pp. ; approbation, &c., 1 p. ;
Latin sub-title, 1 p. ; French sub-title, 1 p. Dedication to Frederick,
Hereditary Prince of Norway, &c., p. 6-19 ; dated, Rostock, 25th
August 1622. The work is in Latin and French, in parallel pages.
                                        —Dr W. Wynn Westcott.

In 16mo, Rome, 1622 ; Rostock, 1623, 8vo. [Lenglet de Fresnoy,
" Histoire de la Philos. Hermit ," 1742, iii. 225, &c.]

The Phœnix " is a creature sacred to the sun, and in
the form of its head and the various tints of its plumage,
distinguished from other birds. All who have described
its characteristics are agreed, but as to the number of years
it lives, accounts vary. The most generally received fixes it
at five hundred years, but there are those who affirm that
one thousand four hundred and sixty-one years intervene
between its visits ; . . having completed his course of
years, on the approach of death builds a nest in his native
land, and upon it sheds a generative power, from which
arises a young one, whose first care, when he is grown up,
is to bury his father. Neither does he go about this task
unadvisedly, but taking up a heavy piece of myrrh, tries
his strength in a long excursion ; and as soon as he finds
himself equal to the burden and passage, he takes his

father's body upon his back, carries it all the way to the altar of the sun, and consumes it in the fire thereon." (Tacitus, "Annals," vi. c. 28.) "They say that he comes from Arabia. . . He hollows out the egg [of myrrh] and puts his parent into it, and stops up with some myrrh the hole through which he had introduced the body. . . . Then, having covered it over, he carries him to the temple of the sun, in Egypt." (Heroditus, "Euterpe," 73.)

This is one of the most curious and rare of Maier's books. Under allegories is given what is most mysterious and hidden in "the great work." The book is in rhymed lines, "and the measure of the anacreonic lines" render the reading "very agreeable." "This singular treatise was first printed at Rome in 1622," the year that Maier died," reprinted at Rostock in 1623, and "since then become very rare." The French edition, the only one I have seen, is issued from Paris, 1758, and is taken from the Rostock edition.

The title promises much—" Nine Triads of Intellectual Songs on the Resurrection of the Phœnix: or the most precious of all medicines, the mirror and abridgement of this Universe, proposed less to the ear than to the mind, and presented to the wise as the key of the three impenetrable Secrets of Chemistry."

The plan and design of the squared Triads :—

1. The names.
2. The allegories.
3. The application of the Mysteries of the Art to those of Religion.

The volume is dedicated to Frederick, Prince of Norway.

In the dedication, Maier speaks of his life spent in study, in mathematics, in all that heaven and earth enclose, seeking also in experiment the knowledge of the practical part of medicine. His care in regard to the study of Hermetic Philosophy cost him incredible labours, at great expense, frequently repeated. He had endured bitter griefs, frequent disappointments.

He gives as the reason of his dedication to Prince
Frederick his known love of learning, that he himself was
a native of Holstein, which he only left fourteen years ago,
to proceed into foreign countries to complete his hermetic
studies. He intends by-and-by to return to Holstein. His
family is well known, not only to all the nobility of Holstein, but also by the Prince's father and grandfather of
happy memory, " to whose service mine have always been
faithfully attached." Maier concludes the dedication by
stating that by-and-by he hopes to offer a work on
medicine of greater importance.

The author then explains his arrangement of songs
alternately—a concert of three voices :—1. Venus ; 2.
Cancer ; 3. Leo.

FIRST TRIAD.

First Part.—Fire—its nature and properties serves as
a cradle for the Phœnix. There it takes a new life. But
this fire is neither that of Etna, Vesuvius, nor Hecla. Our
fire is altogether different ; the origin is from the highest
mountain on earth, which produces only flowers, cinnamon
and saffron. This is the source of all light—it lightens the
Universe, giving light and heat to all beings—never con-
suming. This stake is where the bird goes to seek his
death. It is carefully kept hidden, known only to the
wise. Those who are ignorant of this are ignorant of
all things.

Media.—One hundred voices would not suffice to ex-
press the praise of the Phœnix. Its very ashes find new
vigour in the bosom of death. The Bird is born near
Syene, on the frontiers of Upper Egypt. It has a purple
neck, with a golden collar. Its head is adorned with a
jewel as brilliant as a ruby. Its wings are white without
and deeply red within. Its blood gives it strength, so that
it braves the strongest heat of the sun. It is proof against
fire and water.

Lower.—Thebes is a city of Egypt, with one hundred

gates, and justly conservated to the Sun. The priests most
numerous. They serve that altar on which resides the
divinity of the star which gives light to the Universe.
Delphi, brilliant with the gold of kings, cannot be compared with Thebes. For it is here that, after ten centuries
of life past, in a rapid flight Phœnix goes to find his death,
content to end his days in assurance of renewing his youth.
But in these august funeral rites, no funeral urn is needed,
for scarcely has the Phœnix gone to Thebes than it perishes
in the fire. It is not really the victim of death, but by
unheard-of prodigy, this bird is its own tomb.

SECOND TRIAD.

First Part.—There are different names given to the
fire, and under what allegories the truth lies hidden :—The
celestial dew, most precious ; salt water of the sea, destined
to cook our fish and give it a red tinge : vinegar, which
dissolves every gold, a liquor of sharp taste and bad odour ;
it is called also the water of life, never drying up ; the
menstruum, which gives fertility in the matrix, where the
seed is thrown ; Nature forms the child ; Prometheus'
sacred fire, symbolised by the torches the Bacchantes carried,
the sacred fire burning night and day on the altars of
Vesta and Minerva.

Media.—The Phœnix goes everywhere, over all the
regions of the earth, the highest mountains, the lowest
valleys. It is a vulture, nesting on a tree on the top of a
mountain, and out of its nest comes a raven, calling for
ever for its rights. It is a king engulphed in a deep sea,
seeking to return to his kingdom ; a white Swan, a Peacock, a Pelican in its piety. The double lion, falling to the
ground exhausted ; the serpent wound round the rod of
Mercury.

Lower.—Every place is not suitable for this generation,
nor all urns suitable for the ashes of kings. But a small
part of earth, having a secret virtue, will restore life to
the Phœnix when seemingly dead. I will not betray the

secret, but it is from this earth that the Vase of Hermes is to be formed.

THIRD TRIAD.

First Part.—Of the value of fire in "our art" and in the Universe. Cold retains all in inactivity. But this fire is not by wood; it is almost mineral in nature. All secrets are hid in fire.

Media.—The herb called "Luna." Its stalk is red, its bark blackish; its flower is citron or lemon-coloured. It has a sweet smell, and increased with the phases of the moon. Lullius has under allegories hidden its secret virtues known to all sages. The herb called "Glaucus." It is the famous "Moly" which the son of Maia presented to Ulysses against Circe. The power of the sun and moon are enclosed in this herb. It is the basis of the great art. It is the Loadstone attracting the Iron—a Vapour, a Star.

Lower.—Troy did not yield to arms, but was taken by the cunning of the Greeks. The Ramparts can only be scaled by skill. Imitate the Greek trick, if you wish to find the "Stone." These are the famous apples, which were thrown on the "passage of the light Atalanta." The Son of the Sun only possesses the Fleece.

THE FOURTH TRIAD.

First Part.—A Royal Virgin sent some of her subjects to a distant land to find a husband. They arrived in Upper India by Japan. They found a poorly-clad man of royal blood—a skin of fur covered his body. His hair was as of feathers. He returned with them. The day fixed, the loving pair entered the nuptial bed, Venus lavished her favours, and what a sweet slumber was that which followed.

Media.—The poets say that some fierce animals fell from the moon to the earth. Of these was that furious Lion, rising from the congealed foam of Diana, put to death by Hercules. The fables hide great truths. In this lion's mouth is hidden a thing highly esteemed by sages.

Who will conquer this Lion ? The strength and the club of Hercules are required. Try to know this Lion. He is fed with celestial dew.

Lower—A king, rich in land and gold, had an only daughter. She married and had a son of great beauty, who succeeded his grandfather. He married the daughter of another king. The mother of the prince bestowed her riches on her son, and he became most powerful. Everything became golden.

THE FIFTH TRIAD.

First Part.—The lovely Psyche, fully clothed, sought Cupid. She traversed many countries unable to find him. But she heard he was in Arabia. Cupid's inseparable companion is the God of Fire, intolerable to Psyche. She fears him. She told her daughter what was happening. She is wife and mother of the fugitive.

Media—In the islands of the Indian Sea, the Roc, a bird of a prodigious size, is found. It can carry men and horses through the air. Clutching one day an elephant, the huge mass made him fall to the ground. So he died in the death of his enemy. At that moment a man comes and finishes the killing of the monsters. He skins them, cooks the flesh in an oven to serve as a feast to a king. He arrives and dines on it. This food so strengthens the sight, that through the thickest clouds what is hidden can be perceived. This food then is reserved to bestow wisdom on kings.

Lower.—One of the heirs of Tamerlane reviews his treasuries. He uses immense sums to provide a temple for his father. The sides of it are adorned with a triple row of pillars, which carry their heads to the clouds. The foundations are of gold, so that fire and water may not injure them. The prince believes that his father's soul will dwell there with his body.

The Egyptian Serapis thus passed after death into the precious urn he now inhabits.

THE SIXTH TRIAD.

First Part.—A dragon of immense size inhabits a cave, and spreads his venom on all passers. By his breath many are killed.

Socrates discovered, by concave mirrors, that on a high pillar was hidden a serpent—basilisk—fatal to man. Then on another tower he placed a figure of this monster, that the monster might see it. He added a mirror of metal which, by magnetic virtue, attracted all persons. The basilisk, seeing his image, swallowed the poison without perceiving it. It is a great art to know how to kill this dragon—to take its poison and pass it into polished metals.

Media.—On the cónfines of Persia is the Red Sea, where, after dangers, a vessel from the Teutonic country was by accident driven by winds. The ship bore as its ensign a bounding ox with a star on its forehead, surrounded by a circle of red iron, which was the ship's cargo. The vessel was shipwrecked, and the captain saw the bottom of the sea all scattered with loadstone, drawing to it the vessel laden with iron. The loadstone stops the goddess, whose blood reddens the white rose.

Lower.—The Brachmans told a Prince of Parthia that a time would come when the earth should become barren. They advised him to build vast barns. Workmen accomplished this, and into these he collected all fruits, reserving presents to Bacchus and Ceres. If you find out the meaning of this, you will see its brilliancy. Those who live by the Nile, even the sages, are eager to lay by gold—multiplying gold by gold.

THE SEVENTH TRIAD.

First Part.—This is the Queen of the Sciences. Lullius says it is an abridgment of all arts. The deepest secrets give a lively image of our creation and redemption. Adam was made of red earth and filled with the breath of God. So, also, the sages have their matter of red earth. Three rivers watered Eden, so three streams water our work, and also a subtile dragon, most black.

Media.—All Adam's posterity subjected to death. Then the Creator in mercy remembered him, and resolved to save the human race from death by the greatest of all mysteries. He became man, born of a virgin, shedding His blood, died on the Cross, crushing the head of the dragon, taking away his poison. Lullius, in figures, also displays this mystery. The pure comes to the help of the impure and strengthens metallic sulphur. He who sees how JESUS CHRIST saved us from death will understand the art and the purification and colour of metals.

Lower.—The power of the Eternal is far above reason—has neither beginning nor end. So nothing can be compared with it. God and man were in one Person that He might remedy evil and save Adam's posterity. So the fixed bodies will never unite with the volatile unless there is a sweet bond to bring extremities together. A "Mediator" must be sought. O! Marvels of Nature, what adorable traces do you offer of our Saviour. Thus is Nature called blessed, revealing the mysteries of Divinity.

THE EIGHTH TRIAD.

First Part.—Adam's children carry everywhere the stain of original sin, therefore JESUS CHRIST requires them to be reborn of the Spirit in the Sacred Waters of Baptism. Thus things of Art resolve themselves into liquor for a new birth. Thus after the birth of Bacchus, he was given to nymphs to feed him on water, so that, in the gardens, he might be nourished with dew. He was called Bimater, because his mother gave birth to him twice.

Media.—JESUS CHRIST, raised on the Cross, suffered a cruel death to pay to the Trinity the penalty due to our sins. He received five wounds, whence flowed His innocent blood to wash out our stains. For this His Flesh and Blood are offered on our altars under the species of Bread and Wine, to serve to the faithful as a pledge of salvation.

The sages also offer us an image of this mystery in sacred art. That in it we see streams of blood flowing which, when they penetrate metals, preserve them in violent fires. This blood from Pyramus blackened the fruits of the mulberry, originally white—this from Venus foot reddened the roses, formerly white. He who comes forth empurpled has a perfection incomparable.

Gravis.—The prophet Elias, being carried to heaven in chariot of fire, is a proof of our future life. Enoch also. JESUS CHRIST also proves this by His Resurrection and Ascension. Thus, in an actual picture, the Adept sees the dead arising from the shades of the tomb, for the volatile has preserved their lives amid the strongest flames.

THE NINTH TRIAD.

First Part.—O! adorable Trinity, deep beyond our understanding, how can we celebrate you worthily? A mortal formed of clay cannot conceive Thee. Man cannot raise himself to divine secrets But may I contemplate, through a cloud, the light of this Sun—one only God who formed of nothing all the universe. He is the Father, the Beloved Son—the Spirit of Love proceeding from both. In Art three things very distinct are united by a singular bond which the most violent fire cannot divide:—1. The Paternal Body, the Filial Bond—the Spirit uniting both produces sweet agreement, and no violence can separate the metals.

Media.—That King of Egypt, both Priest and Sage [Hermes] speaks often of Father, Son, and Holy Ghost. From that fact many sages affirm that he was not ignorant of the Incarnation. It is thus that the good Ferrarius has thought. For us we hold what religious teachers, both sacred books and profane authors, tell us. New proofs can be no crime, but written and traced in the books of Nature. A Pure Virgin conceives without man's aid, and gives to the world a male child. He is of three things the only one to be seen without. Seeing the first and last. Who can understand this? Our Virgin in the stars, beside the ass and manger. Her spouse is the Man of Diana, her brother and her son.

Lower.—We cannot know the eternal joys of the future life. "Eye hath not seen, nor ear heard, neither have entered into the heart of man the things which God hath prepared for them that love Him." Man inhabiting this coarse earth cannot understand the marvels of Heaven. The Light of Supreme Being makes our happiness. We shall ever sing untiringly the praises of the Creator. Thence it comes that we seek here what seems nearest heavenly things. Gold is the object of all desires. All nations seek it. It is the Prize and Measure of Nature and Art, because this metal is proof against the violence of fire. Gold alone is durable. So, too, it, in its compact nature, deserves to be compared to Divine and Eternal Things.

A specimen of the Latin verse may be interesting (p. 124) :—

> " Virga pura concipit
> Absque patre, quæ dedit
> Post puellam masculum
> Has in auras splendidum
> Hæc trium res altera
> Visitur, non ultima,
> Nec prior ; quam candido
> Ventre misit e suo
> Virgo mater. O sacra
> Quis capit mysteria."

MICHAELIS MAJERI, Com. Pal. Med. Doct., &c., p.m. Tractatus Posthumus, sive ULYSSES ; hoc est. Sapientia seu Intelligentia, tanquam coelestis scintilla beautitudinis, quod si in fortunæ et corporis bonis naufragium faciat, ad portum meditationis et patientiæ remigio feliciter se expediat. Una cum annexis Tractatibus de Fraternitate Roseæ Crucis. Francofurti Apud Lucam Jennisium, anno MDCXXIV.

8vo ; continuous pagination, 274 ; to end of " Ulysses," p. 41 ; Præfatio ad Lectorem, to page 9.

Affixed :—

I. COLLOQUIUM RHODOSTAUROTICUM trium personatum, Per Famam, et Confessionem, quodammodo revalatum, de Fraternitate Roseæ Crucis, in quo videre est quid tandem de tot, diversisque, ipsorum nomine publicatis scriptis, atque adeo ipsa de Societate statuendum sit. Omnibus fidelibus, et tot scriptis in errorem conjectis, Christianis Lectoribus prælo publico amoris ergo, adornatum. Matth. 5 v. 16. Luceat lux vestra eorum hominibus, ut videant vestra bona opera, et glorificetur Pater vester cælestis. Anno MDCXXIV.

On back of title, " Matth. 24. Et aliquis ex ipsis scriba . . . teipsum," ad Lectorem Theosophicum, 4 pp. ; Copia dictæ illius epistolæ. C. I. B. F. ad me A. S. N. B., 4 pp. ; work, p. 53-161.

II. ECHO COLLOQUII RHODO-STAUROTICI, hoc est.
Resolutio sive Responsio ad nupero tempore editum
trium personarum Colloquium Fraternitatem Roseæ
Crucis concernens. In quo videre est Quo non
Solummodo author dicti illius Colloquii in scribendo
respexit, sed ·etiam quomodo proprie cum Fraternitate ista comparatum sit. Mandato Superiorum
confecta per Bendictum Hilarionem, Fr. Colleg. &c.
Per Angusta ad Augusta, Angustis, Augusta, viis
petit ardua virtus, non datur, ad cælum, currere
lata via. Anno Christi, MDCXXIV.

On back of title :—
Post pluvias formosa dies, Post nubila Phoebus,
Post lacrymas tandem lætior hora venit.
pp. 165-202.

III.—CHRISTIANÆ RELIGIONIS SUMMA, per clar-
issimum virum Joannem Diazium Hispanum.

pp. 205-216. The paper and printing of these pieces are poor,
and there are no illustrations.

IV. SCHOLASTERIUM CHRISTIANUM seu Ludus
credentium, quo tædium horarum seu temporis
molestia abigitur et levatur. Anno MDCXXIV.

pp. 217-274.
—ADVOCATES' LIBRARY, Edinburgh.

This work may be regarded as a sort of memorial
volume to the memory of the deceased. In the preface to
reader, the friend who publishes it refers to Maier as
"quem in vivis adhuc esse certo sibi persuadebant," and
says that his honoured friend, "anni MDCXXII., tempore
æstivo, Magdeburgi naturæ debitum pie persolvisse omnes
et singulos certiores redderem." That, when still alive, he
had given this little work called Ulysses into the hands

of his friend. It being but a small item, the editor has
added to it two other tracts, the " Colloquium " and the
" Echo," both now translated from the German into the
Latin tongue. He then moots the question, Was he, Doctor
Maier, ever the defender of the brotherhood of the Rosy
Cross during his life ? "in ordinem istum receptus fuerit.
Ad hoc me illud nescire, respondeo. Hoc tamen minime
ignoro, quomodo videlicet ad extremum cum ipso quodammodo comparatum fuerit." But whether or not he was
admitted a brother of the Rosy Cross, certain it is that he
was " Religionis Christi, vel Regni Christi Fratrem fuisse,
notum est." He was also, it is to be noted, a regular
attendant at the house of God and a Christian in life and
conversation. He gloried in the profession of religion, and
practised that charity which is exhibited to us in the
person of Christ, as shown in the parable of the good
Samaritan. To love God and his neighbour was his aim, as
it should be that of the reader. The preface is " dabantur
Francofurti ad Mænum." No date is given. The work,
" Ulysses," begins with the statement, no one is happy
except the wise, that yet unhappiness can be turned into
joy, bad transformed to good. It is the mind which deter-
mines our happiness. It is said of Ulysses that, when tried
by ill fortune, he was neither cast down nor turned back
by the breeze, by the rain, by the cold, or by the motion of
the sea. Let us follow in the way of Ulysses—consider his
great gifts, intelligence, and wisdom.

1. Ulysses was a man " astutissimus." He was not
easily deceived, nor did danger or ambush overcome him.
He was guided by truth, virtue, and piety. He had the
eye of the serpent and the heart of the dove. Astute, so
that no foxy ways could deceive him ; others might be
taken in, but even the fox, using a lion's skin as a covering,
could not frighten Ulysses.

2. " Facundia autem Ulyssem imprimis ornavit." In
his speech " pro armis Achillis contra Ajacem," this char-
acteristic is more than once observable.

3. Prudence, as Ovid sang :—

> " Non dubia est Ithaci prudentia sed tamen optat,
> Fumum de patriis posse videre focis."

A prudence seen both in words and deeds, joined with craft transferred to action, and combined with eloquence. This prudence was well seen in his conduct in the Trojan expedition; or, again, when he slew Polyphemus and delivered his companions. Then, too, " Septimo, Sirenes navis malo adalligatus præteriit." His prudence was amply proved by his conduct during his wanderings after the destruction of Troy. Maier cannot pass over the reference to the flower or herb moly, that which had a white flower and a black root—a sweet, lovely flower, but a bitter root. " Per angustas ad augusta, per laborem ad gloriam, per virtutem ad immortale nomen tenditur et pervenitur." This moly is that which is referred to by Gratian the Philosopher " in arte," its beginning miserable and sharp, its end joy and gladness.

The other characteristics of Ulysses. " 4. Ingeniosissimus vir; 5. In bello egregius; 6. In consiliis dandis expeditissimus; 7. Laborum et periculorum patientissimus." Great in war against his enemies, " pro aris et focis, pro parentibus et liberis." There is also a war against wild beasts, the lion and the bear. Hear the song of Ulysses (Ovid, " Metam.," xiii) :—

> " ' My task performed, with praise I had retir'd ;
> But not content with this, to greater praise aspir'd ;
> Invaded Rhesus and his Thracian crew,
> And him and his in their own strength I slew ;
> Returned a victor, all my vows complete,
> With the king's chariot, in his royal seat :
> Refuse me now his arms, whose fiery steeds
> Were promised to the spy for his nocturnal deeds.
>
> .   .   .   .   .   .
> Nor want I proofs of many a manly wound,
> All honest, all before ; believe not me :
> Words may deceive, but credit what you see.'
> At this he bar'd his breast and show'd his scars,
> As of a furrow'd field, well ploughed with wars."

Maier now draws out a simile. The medical man fights with death, but has exactly to know where and how the

danger lies. "Taurina enim non sunt nunc in usu, sed
Leonina quæ astu et strategemate not carent, bella."
Ulysses was the wisest of counsellors, not in frivolous
things, but in those of the greatest moment. See his
constancy against the Cyclops, the Sirens, Tartarus—"Con-
stantissimus est Ulysses." He despises Boreas. In all
kinds of fortune he is equal, and conquers by reason of
his indomitable patience. Ulysses, then, is the symbol of
perfect human wisdom, that wisdom which adorns manners,
gives riches, and tempers virtues. Of its excellences, proof
is given from the Wisdom of Sol. vii. :—"Neither compared
I unto her any precious stone, because all gold in respect of
her is as a little sand, and silver shall be counted as clay
before her." Wisdom, therefore, is greater riches than gold
or silver. Crowns may indeed be the exterior ornaments
of kings, but wisdom is the interior rule by which all
actions of life must be regulated. Wisdom is like the
palm tree--like the clinging, evergreen ivy. It is the
equilateral cube. It is that which brings near to us the
sun, the moon, heaven and earth, annuls distance. Wisdom
has no enemy but ignorance. Pallas, that came from the
brain of Jupiter, was the embodiment of wisdom. Vulcan
and Pallas had but one altar. Wisdom and fire go together.
Wisdom brought forth all useful arts and sciences ; and was
it not Ulysses that

> "from Troy conveyed
> The fatal image of their guardian maid.
> That work was mine."

He found "where the secret lay. But Ulysses was not the
only one who left his fatherland and by long journeys
sought to find out truth and wisdom. Pythagoras, Plato,
Democritus, Homer, Euclid, Apollonius, and innumerable
others sought for knowledge not only in Egypt but in
India. Apollonius of Tyana, gained secrets from the
Brachmans there by arcane magic and sacrifices. Some
even sought the Tartarean region and by most desolate and
difficult wanderings :—

"Illum Scylla rapax canibus subscincta molosis
Ætnæ usque lacus, et squallida tartara torrent."

What Horace sings in his love for Lalage may be better
sung in praise of wisdom :—

> " Place me where never summer breeze
> Unbinds the glebe, or warms the trees ;
> Where ever low'ring clouds appear,
> And angry Jove deforms the inclement year.

> " Place me beneath the burning ray,
> Where rolls the rapid car of day ;
> Love and the nymph shall charm my toils—
> The nymph who sweetly speaks, and sweetly smiles."

Whoever thus will live, with a spark of what is divine
in his mind, can fan it into the flame of wisdom by study
and the exercise of virtue, and spend life, not in lukewarm
perversity and deception (like the most of men), but in the
way of truth, justice, piety, and all virtue, and as life
declines and flows softly away, will near the port of true
tranquility and eternal safety (Christo Salvatore duce), and
there abide for ever. May He light us thither, who is the
Triune, yet one God, blessed for evermore. Amen.

The three treatises affixed to the " Ulysses" are only
interesting to us so far as they refer to " Maier." The
first, the " Colloquium," is a series of conversations on the
Society of the Rosy Cross, by Quirinus, Polydorus, Tyrosophus, Promptutus, and Politicus. Mention is made (p. 93)
by Tyrosophus of the " Symbolum Aureæ Mensæ," in connection with the possibilities of " the Stone," as to the
arcane studies of the " Collegia " in Maier's " Silentium "
(p. 138). A list is afterwards given of approved books—
in theology, Thomas a Kempis, Tauler, Lewis Carbo,
Gerhard, Savanarola ; in chemistry, Trevisan, 12 keys of
Basil, &c.; Robert Castrensis' " Speculum," the works of
Paracelsus and of Agrippa. Again, as to the " habitation "
of the society, Maier is quoted (p. 144), " ex sua Themide
Aurea, pag. 42."

In the " Echo," the passage occurs which has given rise
to the opinion that at length and shortly before his death
Maier was admitted into the Order of the R.C. It occurs

M

(p. 168) where, after enumerating several of the works
of Maier, " vir clarissimus," the writer continues, " quæ
scripta etiam a Domino Authore ipso non frustra scripta
esse debent, sed illum, haud immerito, ante mortem ipsius,
tam ingentibus honorariis, quam non minus singularium
mysteriorum communicatione, beabimus."

The writer (p. 173) declared that neither Luther,
Calvin, or Weigelius, or any others, whatever their names
may be, are to be defended in all things.   It is but human
to err, but the Society teaches heavenly truths and the
right understanding of the Divine Word.   The date at
conclusion of the " Echo " is " mense Martio, anno 1622."
So it must have been issued immediately after the death
of Maier.

More interesting are the " Canones declaratorii " affixed
as " Ergon et Parergon, Fr. C. R."   They are in number ten,
and " define God to be the Eternal Father, incorruptible
fire, and everlasting light, discuss the generation of the
invisible and incomprehensible Word of God, and the
tetradic manifestation of the elements."   (Waite, " Real
Histy.," p. 273.)   " Pater, Filius, Spiritus Sanctus, Spiritus,
Anima, Corpus, Spiritus ab ævo, Ignis, Aqua, Terra, Sulphur,
Mercurius, Sol.

The first three treat of the Persons in the Trinity.   The
fourth relates to the Divine love, " in verbo erat spiritus
super aquam agitans."   The Divine fire is the cause of and
in all motion.   It produces all, and it is the perpetual
connection with the Divine Essence that holds life.   One
hundred and twenty new chemical propositions follow.
For instance, under the name and story of Demogorgon,
are to be seen the material and method " hujus artis " (97).
" The ancient chaos is our Saturn " (98).   By the Phœnix,
which always revives, is to be understood the multiplica-
tion of the Elixir (96).   Under the fables of Hercules and
Antheus we are to see the preparation of the Sulphur (76).
The whole are worthy of study and consideration.   These
propositions are followed by a poem in seven verses.

At page 202 we have the next part—the sum of the Christian religion, by Diaz. This little treatise is of the Reformed or Lutheran faith, admitting, indeed, the three creeds, four general councils, the doctrine of the orthodox fathers, but denying the virtue of the Eucharistic Sacrifice, and granting the admission of clergy by the " ministri " and the civil magistrate, the " Minister or Pastor " being the designation given.

Diaz, a Spaniard, who had embraced the reformed opinions, was murdered at the instance of his own brother, a doctor of the Roman Court, in 1546. The whole tragic story may be read in McCrie, " Reformation in Spain," 87, *et seq.* The treatise here given was first published in French, Lyons, 1562.

IV. The last piece in the collection is the " Scholasterium Christianum." It relates to time, place, eternity ; the age of the world is six thousand years ; the infinity of the heavens—our true fatherland—" nullum corpus sine loco, sicut nullus locus sine corpore ; sic nullum est vacuum in rerum Natura." The nature of Christ's body, of those of angels, that perfect happiness does not relate to what is without us, " sed solum in Deo, in te ipso et non extra te." This little work is divided into ten short chapters.

CONTRIBUTORY WORKS, AND WORKS MENTIONED BY OTHERS, WHICH I HAVE NOT SEEN.

ÆNIGMA.

See Borel (Pierre), "Bibliotheca Chimica," 1654, p. 275 ; mentioned by Ferguson, " Bibl. Chem.," *in voce* Maier.

SUBTILIS ALLEGORIA super Secreta Chymiæ.

See " Musaeum Hermeticum," 1749, p. 701-740 ; mentioned by Ferguson, " Bibl. Chem " ; Gardner, " Bibl. Rosa.," 359 ; also by L. du Fresnoy, " Hist. de la Philosophie Hermetique," iii. *in voce* Maier.

TREUHERTZIGE WARNUNGS VERMAHNUNG
an alle wahre Liebhaber der Naturgemafsen Alchymiæ transmutatoriæ.

See Rothscholtz (Friederich), " Deutsches Theatrum Chemicum," 1728, i. p. 289 ; Tharsander, "Adeptus Ineptus," 1744, p. 95 ; quoted by Ferguson, " Bib. Chem," *in voce*.

EMBLEMATA NOVA CHEMICA.

In 4to ; Oppenheimii, 1618 ; quoted by Du Fresnoy, and by Gardner, " Bibl. Rosicruciana," No. 345.

DE ROSÆ-CRUCE.

4to ; Francofurti, 1618 ; quoted by Gardner, " Bibl. Rosa.," No. 344 ; Du Fresnoy.

ENCOMIUM MERCURII—In Amphitheatro Sapientiæ et Stultitiæ, Caspar Dornavius.

Folio, Danielis et Davidis Aubriorum, Hanoviæ, 1619 ; *vide* pp. 604, *et seq. ;* quoted by Du Fresnoy, and by Gardner, " Bibl. Rosa.," 346.

MUSEUM CHEMICUM.

In 4to ; Francof., 1708, "avec figures" ; quoted by Du Fresnoy.

MAIERU (M.) VOM EGERISCHEN SCHLEDER SAWERBRONNEUS.

12mo ; Nürnberg, 1637 ; quoted by Gardner, " Bibl. Rosa.," No. 355.

ECHO FRATERNITATIS ROSEÆ CRUCIS, Dantisci, 1616.

8vo ; " has been attributed" to Maier ; Ferguson, " Bibl. Chem."

COMITIA PHILOSOPHICA.

Mentioned by Kopp ; Ferguson, " Bibl. Chem."

MICHAELIS MEYERI, D. VIRIDARIUM CHYMICUM, DAS IST : CHYMISCHES LUST GARTLEIN, in sich begrieffend etlich und fünffzig Philosophische Sinnenbilder, deren Beschriebung in teutsche Reimen gefasset, durch einen Liebhaber deren Wissenschafft. Franckfurt am Mayn, Bey Herman von Sand. MDCLXXXVIII.

Oblong 8vo ; 112 pp. ; title ; preface, pp. 3-6 ; p. 7 blank ; p. 8, verses ; p. 9, copperplate engraving, and thereafter verses on the *verso*, and engraving on the *recto* of each page. Compare Stolcius de Stolcenberg's book. Copy in Dr Young's Library, and description from Ferguson's " Bibl. Chem.," *in voce* Maier.